THE PRESIDENTS SPEAK:
Addresses from the Leadership of the
East Texas Historical Association, 2000-2016

THE PRESIDENTS SPEAK:
Addresses from the Leadership of the East Texas Historical Association, 2000-2016

edited by
Milton S. Jordan and Dan K. Utley

STEPHEN F. AUSTIN STATE UNIVERSITY PRESS

Copyright © 2017 Milton S. Jordan and Dan K. Utley

All rights reserved. Printed in the United States of America. No part of this book may be used or reproduced in any manner whatsoever without writen permission except in the case of brief quotations in critical articles or reviews.

For more information:
Stephen F. Austin State University Press
P.O. Box 13007 SFA Station
Nacogdoches, Texas 75962
sfapress@sfasu.edu
www.sfasu.edu/sfapress

Distributed by Texas A&M Consortium
www.tamupress.com

ISBN: 978-1-62288-178-9

With great admiration and appreciation, this work is dedicated to all East Texas Historical Association officers—past, present, and future—whose selfless contributions of time and talents set high standards for promoting regional history and an abiding sense of place.

Contents

Foreword by Portia Gordon . . . i
Introduction . . . iii
Acknowledgments. . . v

PART ONE: The ETHA Presidents, 1962-2016 . . . 1

PART TWO: The Presidential Speeches, 2000-2016

"Jane McManus Storm Cazneau and the Galveston Bay and Texas Land Company" . . . 9
    LINDA S. HUDSON

"Writing Coffee Table History Without Getting Verklempt: Fort Worth and the New Frontier" . . . 28
    TY CASHION

"The Civil Rights Bill of 1964: One Small Town's Contribution" . . . 32
    GAIL K. BEIL

"East Texas and African American History: The Past and the Future" . . . 46
    CARY WINTZ

"R.L. Moore: Legendary Mathematician and Teacher" . . . 55
    R.G. DEAN

"Steve Allen Never Picked Cotton in Texas" . . . 65
    DAN K. UTLEY

"Journey from Tampa to Dallas to Nacogdoches" . . . 80
    THEORDORE LAWE

"A River Creeps Through It" . . . 84
    MILTON S. JORDAN

"Is Our Collective Memory Folklore or History?" . . . 90
    TOM CRUM

"The Evolution of Memory in a Small Texas Town: Janis Joplin and Port Arthur" ... 96
    CYNTHIA J. BEEMAN

"Anti-Black Violence in Twentieth-Century East Texas" ... 106
    BRUCE A. GLASRUD

"East Texas and the Battle for Texas' Past" ... 118
    GENE PREUSS

"Bound for Beaumont: Eleanor Roosevelt's 1939 Train Trip through East Texas and Beyond" ... 131
    MARY L. SCHEER

"The Long Journey of Joshua Louis Hicks: A Voice from the Texas Working Class" ... 144
    KYLE WILKISON

Foreword

In 1995, my husband, Charlie, and I moved to Nacogdoches, where I initially worked for a temporary service. When I decided to seek permanent employment, Stephen F. Austin State University was hiring. My first interview was with Dr. Archie McDonald, a history professor and director of the East Texas Historical Association (ETHA). Following my second interview with him, he looked at me and said, "Do you want this job?" I said, "Yes," and that was the start of a great team. I went through the usual orientation with Stephen F. Austin State University and then realized the school would be my employer rather than the association. ETHA, though, became the most valuable position with an extended family, including Dr. McDonald, I could possibly ever have.

My first meeting with ETHA was in September 1995 at the Fredonia Hotel in Nacogdoches. I was nervous and lost as a goose about how things worked, but thanks to Pat Kell, a member and future ETHA president (1998-1999), for the assistance and directions she gave me. Cissy Lale, who served as president (1994-1995) for the meeting, was the wife of Max S. Lale, a former president (1981-1982) of the association. Max was the donor for the Georgiana and Max S. Lale Lectures and brought noted speakers, such as Bill Moyers, Charlie Wilson, and Jeff Guinn to the university campus. In fact, after Max's death, the East Texas Historical Journal (Spring 2007) had a special issue dedicated in his memory.

On occasion the reigning president would invite the association to hold the spring meeting at a special location. Ted Lawe (2008-2009), the first African American president, invited the association to Emory, where the McMillan African American Museum he co-directed is located. I do believe the favorite location for the spring meetings was always Galveston, at the rather luxurious Tremont House, where the weather was decently comfortable and the seafood outstanding.

For thirteen years, I met some very interesting people as secretary/treasurer of the association and worked closely with all the presidents during that time. Some of them were lay historians, history professors, museum curators, and public schoolteachers. They also included a former mayor, a mathematics professor, and retired judge. Each year, Dr. McDonald would make suggestions to include different vocations for the nominating committee tasked with filling slates of officers and board members for upcoming terms. In that regard, he maintained a strong influence on the leadership through the years. He would always have a suggested itinerary for the incoming president and other officers, and would spend considerable time with them, making suggestions for programs and projects, and discussing goals for the coming year.

One of Dr. McDonald's special names for one of the presidents was the "Marlboro Man"—it just happened to be his dear friend, Ken Henrickson, Jr., the president for 2001-2002. There were other presidents who impressed Dr. McDonald because they had been his students, and of course he gave special attention to them as well. Those I remember in particular were Joe L. White (1986-1987), Virginia Long (1987-1988), Linda Cross (1989-1990), Linda S. Hudson (2000-2001), and Gail K. Beil (2003-2004).

I remember one of the presidential addresses very well. The speech about "pickin' cotton in Texas" was given by future president Cynthia J. Beeman (2011-2012), but actually in place of its author, Dan K. Utley (2006-2007), who, in an emergency, left his gallbladder in Round Rock instead of attending the fall meeting in Nacogdoches. I remember other addresses as notable, including those of Tom Crum (2010-2011), who gave his Friday night address about history and folklore, and Milton Jordan (2009-2010), who made parallels about history and East Texas rivers. All of the presidential papers have been memorable and notable in their own rights.

The East Texas Historical Association has a long history of having a great group of presidents. F. Lee Lawrence was the first president. Dr. C.K. Chamberlain, a history professor at Stephen F. Austin State University, which has housed and supported the association since its founding, was the first director and editor before Dr. McDonald took over in 1971, serving for thirty-seven years before Dr. Scott Sosebee came on board. There is much to celebrate about the history of the ETHA, and its presidents have served as an integral team in that regard. It is thus fitting that we celebrate their diverse interests as reminders of their service and as reflections of the noteworthy scholarship they shared with all of us.

Portia L. Gordon
Secretary, East Texas Historical Association, 1995-2008

Introduction

F. Lee Lawrence, a Tyler attorney, F. I. Tucker, an attorney from Nacogdoches, and C.K. Chamberlain, Chair of the History Department at Stephen F. Austin State University called the organizational meeting of the East Texas Historical Association at the Nacogdoches school in September 1962. Those attending that gathering selected Chamberlain as editor/director and Lawrence as the first president. One year later, Tucker became president of the association. From 1963 through the end of the century, thirty-seven men and women served one-year terms as president. Throughout those years, the presidents often presented papers at association meetings during their terms in office. They were not called on, however, to offer presidential addresses, a custom that formally began with the new century.

In September 2001, at the close of her term, Pres. Linda Hudson delivered a presidential address for the East Texas Historical Association's Friday evening banquet. At each of the following fifteen fall meetings, the association president has delivered the banquet address. The majority of these presidents have been professional historians employed by colleges or universities, historical commissions, or other similar agencies. A few worked in other fields, but they all shared an avid interest in the history of the East Texas region.

The professional and avocational historians alike had a common concern—that association members and others come to know more fully the stories of the people, events, and places that make East Texas its own particular—even peculiar—region. Their presidential addresses seek to work out that concern through a variety of forms. Some explored individual lives within varying contexts of history, while others chose to weave in aspects of their personal stories and experiences as they reflected on the regional context. All of the presentations, in their varied ways, address the hope that their audience continues to seek out and make known the stories of East Texas history.

We have found much enjoyment in editing these addresses of association presidents and we thank everyone who helped provide them. In most cases this involved time and effort in searching out notes and manuscripts from years in the past, and for some a bit of reconstruction or reflection.

Introduction

This book includes thirteen of the original sixteen presidential addresses, with some modifications, documentation, and enhancements for publication purposes. One additional paper represents a contemporaneous article the editors chose to include in lieu of the presidential address, which is no longer available. Regrettably, two other presidential addresses were simply not available for this book, which speaks to one of our purposes in starting on this project. It is our sincere hope that *The Presidents Speak* will serve as a call for the long-term systematic preservation and publication of ETHA presidential addresses—and indeed those of other organizations—as a means of bequeathing a more complete record of associational scholarship and leadership insights to future generations. Historians, after all, should set the example of chronicling the past, even their own contributions to that past.

Acknowledgments

This book represents the hard work and partnership of many people. First and foremost are the presidents whose papers are included herein. It is their research, writing, and insights that form the backbone of this work, and we greatly appreciate their willingness to share their papers again with an even wider audience. Additional thanks are due to those who helped preserve some of the papers in various forms as previously published works. They include Texas A&M University Press, the East Texas Historical Association, and the Texas Gulf Coast Historical Society. We are indebted as well to Gwen Lawe for providing a copy of the address delivered by her late husband and our friend, Ted Lawe.

Once again, we find ourselves in debt to Portia Gordon, longtime—and now retired—secretary of the East Texas Historical Association, who provided invaluable background information for this project and graciously contributed a foreword to set the context. She is one of the true "rocks" of the organization, and we would never have been able to proceed without her kind assistance, which is always given with great humor and enthusiasm. Also providing important associational support to the editors was director M. Scott Sosebee, who has worked closely with many of the authors/presidents represented in this compilation and helped publish some of the more recent works. To him and the association directors will fall the responsibility of developing a system for the future preservation and utilization of presidential addresses to ensure a comprehensive record from this point forward.

Our special thanks to an important member of our team, Kimberly Verhines, who, as editor of Stephen F. Austin State University Press, provided us with encouragement and support. Jerri Bourrous at the press has been especially helpful with design and editing. We are honored to be distantly-related members of the SFA family, many of whom have, at various levels, worked diligently to ensure the greater story of East Texas endures into the future.

We have enjoyed partnering again on behalf of our beloved East Texas Historical Association, which we have both served as presidents. We close this section where we began, thanking our esteemed collegial leaders from the past, but this time also including those who will guide the organization in the years ahead. To the latter in particular, we hope the words of those who came before will serve as inspiration and as a never-ending source of a proud and shared heritage. Onward.

Milton S. Jordan
Dan K. Utley
May 2017

PART ONE:
The Presidents, 1962-2017

East Texas Historical Association Presidents

Fifty-four individuals served as presidents of the East Texas Historical Association (ETHA) from 1962 to 2016. Each served one-year terms, usually after two years in preparation as vice president, and then an additional two years on the baord of directors for continuity. Information on each of the presidents is included here along with a brief note on their life and profession at the time of their tenure.

F. Lee Lawrence (1962-1963), a Tyler attorney, led in the formation of the ETHA. He and history professor Dr. C.K. Chamberlain called the initial meeting at Stephen F. Austin State College in Nacogdoches on September 29, 1962, and Lawrence became the first association president. Later, he received the Ralph W. Steen Award for Distinguished Service.

F.I. Tucker (1963-1964), a Nacogdoches attorney, became the second president at the general membership fall meeting held in Nacogdoches, as it was each year through 2016. Tucker was an avid student of East Texas history and dedicated to historic preservation.

Seth Walton (1964-1965), a history professor at East Texas Baptist College in Marshall, presided over and presented a paper at the association's first spring meeting in Jefferson in 1963. He was the first professional historian to serve as president and later received the Ralph W. Steen Award.

Robert W. Glover (1965-1966), a graduate of Stephen F. Austin State College, served as professor of history at Tyler Junior College. His monograph, Camp Ford, CSA, was one of the association's first publications. He was a Steen Award recipient and an ETHA Fellow.

Alan C. Ashcraft (1966-1967) was a history professor at Texas A&M University. His particular interest was the Civil War in the Southwest. Ashcraft's article on the scope of East Texas, published in the East Texas Historical Journal, was one of the earliest and most successful efforts to define the region.

Ralph A. Wooster (1967-1968) was a professor of history at Lamar University in Beaumont. He is a Fellow of the association and received the Steen Award and the Otis Lock Award for excellence in teaching.

Terrell W. Connor (1968-1969) was a native of Daingerfield and a longtime employee of General Dynamics in numerous locations.

C.M. Langford (1969-1970), a native of Henderson and judge of the Rusk County Commissioners Court, was the first elected public official to serve as association president.

James L. Nichols (1970-1971), professor of history at Stephen F. Austin State College, was instrumental in selecting Archie P. McDonald as association director, a position McDonald held for thirty-seven years. Nicholls received the Outstanding Faculty Award at SFA and the Steen Award.

Robert C. Cotner (1971-1972) began his career as a Texas public schoolteacher and served as dean of men at Henderson State University and Stetson University before joining the faculty of the University of Texas at Austin, where he served for thirty-five years. He received the association's Steen Award.

Ralph Goodwin (1972-1973) was professor of history at East Texas State College, now Texas A&M University-Commerce, where he directed the honors program. He was present at the organizing meeting of the association in September 1962.

Robert S. Maxwell (1973-1974) was a history professor at Stephen F. Austin State College with a special focus on the East Texas lumber industry. He was a Fellow of the association and one of the first recipients of the Steen Award.

Maury Darst (1974-1975) was a history professor at Galveston College, a fourth generation Texan whose great grandfather participated in the Battle of San Jacinto.

Charles K. Phillips (1975-1976) taught in the College of Business at Stephen F. Austin State University. He was active in historic preservation and served as chair of the Nacogdoches County Historical Commission. He was a recipient of the Steen Award.

Claude H. Hall (1976-1977), a history professor at Texas A&M University, was the first in that school's liberal arts department to receive the Association of Former Students Distinguished Teaching Award.

Fred Tarpley (1977-1978) wrote the study, *Jefferson: East Texas Metropolis*, an early publication in the Ann and Lee Lawrence Monograph Series. He was a professor at East Texas State University and later at Jarvis Christian College, and a Fellow of the association.

Ralph W. Steen (1978-1979) was president of Stephen F. Austin State College in 1962 when the association organized, and he proved to be essential to its successful beginning. He retired as president of the school in 1976 and two years later, without having served in the vice- presidential positions, became the association president. The distinguished service award is named in his honor.

Frank H. Smyrl (1979-1980) was professor of history at East Texas State College and later a dean at the University of Texas at Tyler. He was a Fellow of the association and received the Ottis Lock Award.

Marion Holt (1980-1981), the first female president of the association, was a professor of history at Lamar University, Beaumont.

Max B. Lale (1981-1982) was a newspaper editor, publisher and public relations officer. He was an ardent supporter of historic preservation and chaired the Harrison County Historical Commission. His generous gift to the association established the Lale Lecture Series. He was a Fellow of the association and recipient of the Steen Award.

Irvin M. May (1982-1983) was a professor of history at Blinn College in Brenham and College Station. He regularly offered his best Texas history students gift memberships in the association. May was a Fellow of the association and received the Steen and Lock Awards.

Bob Bowman (1983-1984) owned and managed a Lufkin public relations firm and founded a publishing house specializing in East Texas history. He was a Fellow of the association, recipient of the Lock and Steen Awards, and a commissioner of the Texas Historical Commission.

William J. Brophy (1984-1985) was a history professor at Stephen F. Austin State University, chair of the History Department, and dean of the College of Liberal Arts. He later served as interim president of the university. A recipient of the Steen Award, the University Academic Enrichment Center is named in his honor.

Jewel Cates (1985-1986) served as a postal telegraph supervisor and airline dispatcher during World War II. She was one of the first women account executives for Merrill Lynch.

Joe L. White (1986-1987) served as president during the association's 25th Anniversary. He was a professor of history at Kilgore College and Director of the East Texas Oil Museum on that campus. White had been an SFA undergraduate when the association formed and later received his master's degree as a graduate assistant for Dr. C.K. Chamberlain, an association founder.

Virginia Long (1987-1988) was a native of Kilgore and a graduate of Kilgore College and the University of Texas at Tyler. She also studied at Stephen F. Austin State University and served as Managing Trustee of the Long Trusts, a benefactor of the association. Interested in historic preservation, she served as a commissioner of the Texas Historical Commission.

Gwin Morris (1988-1989) was professor of history at Wayland Baptist College and later academic dean and Executive Vice President at East Texas Baptist College in Marshall.

Linda Cross (1989-1990), an MA graduate of Stephen F. Austin State University, was a history professor at Tyler Junior College. She received an Ottis Lock research grant and the Steen Award.

Ron Hufford (1990-1991) was executive vice president of the Texas Forestry Association in Lufkin and recipient of the Steen Award.

Bill O'Neal (1991-1992), history professor at Panola College and a Fellow of the association, received the Ottis Lock and Steen awards. He later served as Texas State Historian.

Audrey Kariel (1992-1993) was mayor of Marshall for seven years and an ardent supporter of historic preservation in Harrison County.

Ray Stephens (1993-1994) was professor of history at the University of North Texas and editor of the Internet commentary, *H-Texas*.

Cissy Stewart Lale (1994-1995), a newspaper reporter and editor for several Texas dailies, received the Steen Award and was named a Life Director of the association.

Cecil Harper (1995-1996) was a professor of history at Lone Star College in Houston.

Carol Riggs (1996-1997) was Director of the Texas Forestry Museum in Lufkin and recipient of the Steen Award.

James V. Reese (1997-1998) was professor of history and later Vice President of Academic Affairs at Stephen F. Austin State University. A Fellow of the association, he received the Steen Award.

Patricia Kell (1998-1999), a teacher and administrator in the Goose Creek Consolidated Independent School District at Baytown, received the Steen Award.

Donald E. Willett (1999-2000), history professor at Texas A&M University, Galveston, received the Lock and Steen awards.

Linda S. Hudson (2000-2001) was a professor of history at Kilgore College, Panola College, and East Texas Baptist University. A Fellow of the association, she received three Lock research grants and the C.K. Chamberlain Award.

Kenneth E. Hendrickson, Jr. (2001-2002), the Hardin Distinguished Professor of History at Midwestern State University, received the Thomas L. Charlton Lifetime Achievement Award from the Texas Oral History Association. A Fellow of the association, he received the Lock and Chamberlain awards.

Ty Cashion (2002-2003) was a professor of history at Sam Houston State University and is a Fellow of the association.

Gail K. Beil (2003-2004), a reporter for the *Marshall News Messenger*, received her M.A. in history from Stephen F. Austin State University, where she later taught. She is a recipient of the Lock and Steen awards

Cary Wintz (2004-2005) was a professor of history at Texas Southern University and a Fellow of the association.

R. G. Dean (2005-2006) was a professor of mathematics at Stephen F. Austin State University and established the association's first website. He received the Steen Award.

Dan K. Utley (2006-2007), an editor of this volume, was Chief Historian of the Texas Historical Commission. A recipient of the Steen and Lock awards, he later became a Fellow of the association.

Beverly Rowe (2007-2008) was a professor of history at Texarkana College and active in historic preservation. She received the Steen Award.

Theodore Lawe (2008-2009) was the association's first African American president. A Fellow of the association, he was director of the South Fair Community Development Corporation in Dallas and a founder and director of the A.C. McMillan African American Museum in Emory.

Milton S. Jordan (2009-2010), an editor of this volume, was a retired United Methodist minister and bookseller living in Georgetown. He received the Lock Award and became a Fellow of the association.

Tom Crum (2010-2011) of Granbury became president without serving as vice president due to a resignation in the association leadership. He was a retired state district judge and former president of the West Texas Historical Association.

Cynthia J. Beeman (2011-2012) served as president during the association's 50th Anniversary. She was director of the History Programs Division of the Texas Historical Commission and a board member of the Ruthe Winegarten Memorial Foundation for Texas Women's History.

Bruce A. Glasrud (2012-2013) was emeritus professor of history at California State University, East Bay, and retired dean of Sul Ross State University in Alpine. Glasrud is a Fellow of the association and former president of the West Texas Historical Association.

Gene B. Preuss (2013-2014) was a professor of history at the University of Houston, Downtown.

Mary L. Scheer (2014-2015) was a history professor and chair of the Department of History at Lamar University, and a Fellow of the association.

Kyle G. Wilkison (2015-2016) was a professor of history at Collin College in Plano. He is a Fellow of the association.

PART TWO:
The Presidential Addresses

Jane McManus Storm Cazneau and the Galveston Bay and Texas Land Company

Linda S. Hudson

Although several publications focus on her activities during the Mexican-American War, little has been written about Jane Cazneau's early years in Texas or her experiences with the Galveston Bay and Texas Land Company.[2] Jane Maria Eliza McManus was born April 6, 1807, near Troy, New York. Her parents, William and Catherine Coons McManus, a local politician and his wife, were of New York Irish and Palatine pioneer stock that had migrated to British America decades before the French and Indian War and settled along the Hudson River. Her formal education began at age five under the direction of Sarah Starr in Connecticut. In 1823, she entered Emma Willard's Troy Female Seminary, but instead of completing her studies married Allen B. Storm in 1825, and they had a son, William M. Storm, the following year. For reasons that remain unknown, the couple moved to New York City, where the marriage failed. In 1832, Jane McManus, using her maiden name, kept books for Anthony Dey, director of the Galveston Bay and Texas Land Company. Women did not typically work in offices at that time, but the names and addresses of the Galveston Bay and Texas Land Company stockholders, the amount of stock they held, and company expenses were entered in Jane's distinctive handwriting. According to witnesses, she visited Aaron Burr's office in the evenings where she translated promotional materials on Texas into the German language.[2]

Alarmed at the influx of Americans into Texas, the Mexican government had restricted immigration from the United States with the Law of April 6, 1830, and only Europeans or Mexicans were to settle in Texas. In October 1830, Dey had combined the *empresario* grants of an American, David G. Burnet, a German, Joseph Vehlein, and a Mexican, Lorenzo de Zavala, and formed the Galveston Bay and Texas Land Company. Dey's company, consisting of financial backers from New York and Boston, controlled thirteen million acres covering twenty present-day East Texas counties in an area that stretched from Louisiana westward to the Brazos River and from the Gulf of Mexico to north of Nacogdoches. Although it was illegal under Mexican law, company representatives sold land scrip for five cents an acre to prospective settlers who reserved the right to settle a certain number of acres within the area. The Mexican government had issued the Vehlein grant and the Austin and Williams grant that replaced the expired Robert Leftwich grant for German immigrants. Lorenzo de Zavala, stockholder and Mexican minister to France, promoted Texas land to prospective German, Swiss, and French colonists.

In September and October 1832, Jane McManus and her younger brother, Robert, purchased Galveston Bay and Texas Land Company scrip. Robert's certificates were went to Troy in care of a family friend, United States Senator William L. Marcy. Jane McManus then proposed to the company trustees that she sell scrip in England and Ireland while Robert served as company agent and surveyor in Texas. Dey issued her a power of attorney to do so, but the other trustees, William H. Sumner and George Curtis, rejected her offer. They recommended that Robert be hired as a surveyor for George N. Nixon, the company's agent in Nacogdoches.[3]

The list of Galveston Bay and Texas Land Company stockholders did not include Aaron Burr or Jane's father, William McManus, but contains other familiar persons.[4]

STOCKHOLDERS IN GALVESTON BAY AND TEXAS LAND COMPANY

NAME	ADDRESS	SHARES
Allen, Moses	47 Wall	10
Allen, Gilbert	51 Wall	10
Anthone, Theoppiley	240 Front	2
Austin, Thomas (T.E. Davis)	–	5
Axtell, Dan'l C.	–	8
Bates, George	221 Hudson	1
Beale, Benjamin (C. Edwards)	–	2
Bignall, David	146 Broadway	4
Blake, George	–	1
Boller, Peter	–	2
Bolles, William B.	– Wall	1
Bonney, Benjamin W.	63 Cody	22
Booth, Wm. A.	124 Front St.	1
Booth & Atterbury	Exchange Pl.	1
Bortol, Barnaby	53 West	8
Boswell, Hartwell	–	2

NAME	ADDRESS	SHARES
Buckner, Wm. G.	42 Wall St.	20
Bullock, Moulton	14 Wall	20
Burrill, Alonza, M.	5 Broad	1
Bushnell, Orsamy	3 Napoleon	1
Campbell, Duncan P.	57 Broadway	5
Catlin, Chas. T.	5 Broad	4
Catlin, Lynde (J.M. Wilkinson)	–	7
Clarkson, David	49 Wall	4
Clute, John D.	182 Pearl	1
Cramer, John	143 Mercer	1
Crownshield, Jacob	34 Hudson	7
Currier, John	–	20
Curtis, Geo. & Edward	17 Hanover	10
Curtis, George	17 Hanover	2
Daber, Phillip	161 Front St.	1
Dart, Russell	123 Mayfair Ln.	2
Davis, Thos. E.	42 Wall	10
DeForest, Chas.	Grand Gorge, NY	10
Dey, Catherine A.	–	8
Dey, Anthony	63 Admiral	66
Edwards, Charles	– page damaged	
Enero (sp?), John	– page damaged	
Ferris, John Thomas	378 Greenwich	5
Graham, John L.	–	"
Graham, David	34 Beekman	"
Gray, Maria	86 South	"
Gregory, Dudley L.	3 Courthouse	"
Griswold, George	86 South	"
Griswold, Cornelia W.	86 South	"
Griswold, George, Jnr.	86 South	"
Griswold, Nathan L.	86 South	page damaged
Haggerty, John	Pearl & Pine	8
Hamilton, Alex., Jr.	24 Broad St.	1
Harbun, A.B.	42 Wall	8
Hart, Jim Phillip	22 South St.	1
Hayes, Newbon	197 Broadway	2
Hemingway, Luke	3 Courthouse	4
Henrique, J.M.	42 Wall	4
Henry, Alex.	–	–
Hurd, Jesse	–	3

NAME	ADDRESS	SHARES
Jackson, Henry	–	8
Jennings, N.J.	31 Nassau	10
Lee, David	141 Front Street	11
Lord, Nathaniel	30 Broad St.	39
Lucket, Levin	–	2
Luckett, Alfred	–	2
Manning, Jeremiah	35 Front	1
Marsh, Leonard	159 Suffock	1
Mead, Walker	25 Wall	10
Mexia, Jos. Ant. (Treat)	–	3
Miller, Henry	–	2
Monson, Marcena	32 Varick	33
Munroe, Jr., James	73 Murrey	3
Nelson, James	–	8
Nevins, Refsell	Wall	5
Nevins, Rufus L.	Wall	4
Noland, Wm.	–	4
Oliver, Francis J.	–	10
Packard, Issac (D. Selden)	–	10
Perkins, Cyrus	13 Barclay	2
Poinsett, Joel (Treat)	–	10
Ratalje?, Jeronimus E.	42 Green	2
Rebout, John B.	–	1
Richards, Nathaniel	149 Chambers	8
Russel, Ruth A.	–	4
Russell, Isreal	26 Front	1
Sedwick, Roderick	–	5
Shaw, Latimer R.	125 Pearl	1
Sill, Horace A.	87 South	22
Slacker, John	–	8
Smith, Charles	–	5
Smith, Herman	86 South	3
Smith, Wm. Sidney	–	3
Spofford & Tileson	149 Water	8
St. John, Jr., Saml.	–	5
Sumner, Wm. H.	–	28
Swartwout, Saml.	Custom House	1
Thompson, James (G. Curtis)	–	1
Thorne, Jonathan	14 Jacob	5
Tibbits, Elisha	–	5

NAME	ADDRESS	SHARES
Tomlinson, Wm. A.	124 Front	1
Treadwell, Daniel	–	3
Treat, Chauncey (J. Treat)	–	2
Treat, James	42 Wall	10
Van Dyke, Jas	–	10
Vehlein, Joseph	123 Liberty Ave	page damaged
Wall, Garriot D.	–	"
Whitney, Stephen	71 Front	30
Wilder, S.V.S.	13 Exchange	1
Woodhull, Caleb	184 Water	10
Woodward, John	19 Platt	3
Zavala, Lorenzo de (Treat)	–	85

The exact nature of the relationship between Jane McManus and Aaron Burr where Texas lands were concerned may never be known. Burr and her father were fraternal brothers and political allies, and Dey did have scrip and a guidebook printed in the German language. *Texas und Einlandung zu einer vortheilhaften Unsiedelung daselbt* (1835), by a Mexican citizen, offered the advantages of settlement in Texas. The pamphlet directed Germans to sail from LeHavre to New Orleans, up the Mississippi River to the Red River, then across the Texas border to Nacogdoches, where they exchanged their scrip for land claims.[5]

Personal circumstances first brought Jane McManus and her brother, Robert, to Texas. In 1832, Jane's grandmother, Mary McManus, made her will, and at eighty-one years of age did not mention Jane—a grandchild who she once paid to have the best education available. The omission may have been to prevent Allen Storm from laying claim to his wife's inheritance. In Texas, Spanish Law allowed married women to own separate property, unlike New York, where everything a woman had—land, salary, or children—became the property of her husband upon marriage to sell, control, or squander. Perhaps it was Burr who advised the twenty-five-year-old Jane to come to Texas. Before she sailed from New York in November 1832, Burr suggested that her enterprise had "the air of Romance and Quixotteism [sic]," but he added that it was not without precedent. He reminded her of the young Rhode Island woman, Jemima Wilkinson, who began a similar colony in western New York and helped the United States lay claim to land deep in British-held territory.[6]

In New Orleans, Jane and Robert McManus met Burr's former partner in intrigue, Judge James Workman. A former resident of Charleston, Workman had been a member of the Mexican Association, which he, Louis Kerr, David Clark, and Edward Livingston organized after the Louisiana Purchase did not include Texas. The 300-member group planned to liberate Texas from Spain. Burr, Workman, Burr's secretary Samuel Swartwout, and others were tried for treason in 1807 but acquitted. Burr's recruits then settled on land in Arkansas and Louisiana that acquired by Phillip Enrique Neri, the Baron de Bastrop. In 1821, the baron assisted Moses Austin in obtaining the empresario grant in Texas for 300 Louisiana settlers that led to the Anglo settlement of Texas. Officially, Judge Workman translated Louisiana Spanish law written in the French language into English for American judges to interpret.[7]

In his letter to Workman, Burr introduced Jane McManus as "A Lady!" and "a woman of business." Burr assured Workman that she could "send out one or two hundred substantial settlers in less time . . . than any man or half a Dozen men whom I this day Know." Burr explained that she was her family's agent, and he requested that Workman write her letters of introduction. Burr invited Workman to form his opinion of "her talents and of her competency." Burr thought she was "eminently qualified" and had "that peculiar discernment or tact in the Character and disposition's of men—a talent peculiar to her sex." She "also had (which is more rare) courage, Stability and perseverance. . . . But enough," Burr advised, "Judge for yourself and act accordingly." Workman wrote contacts in Texas to expect the New Yorkers. In December 1832, the siblings arrived in Texas. Jane McManus then purchased from Samuel Sawyer his power of attorney to locate an eleven-league Mexican land grant. Sawyer had obtained the grant from Benjamin Lundy, who had planned to settle free blacks from the United States in Texas.[8]

At the time of Jane's arrival, Samuel May Williams, Stephen F. Austin's partner in settling the area of the original Leftwich Grant, had ordered the surveys of nineteen unlocated eleven-league grants including that purchased by McManus. Unbeknown to Jane, Sterling C. Robertson had arrived from Tennessee and was taking depositions from settlers to prove the Leftwich area was not unsettled when reassigned to Austin and Williams. That same month, Sam Houston came to parley with Comanches and investigate Indian migration to Texas. Some 5,000 Creeks had arranged with the Galveston Bay company to purchase land near Nacogdoches.[9]

Williams and another partner, John Austin, located the eleven-league grants of 48,712 acres for fifty pesos per league plus surveying fees. On January 22, 1833, Charles Sayre, a native of New York, informed Williams that the "New York Commission" was in Brazoria and two weeks later wrote that Mrs. McManus was visiting San Felipe to finalize a purchase. He was "much pleased with her," and described her as "a very intelligent Lady." Sayre urged Williams to hurry the forms because she wished to return to New Orleans with Captain Samuel Fuller, who transported trade goods to Texas and hides and cotton back to New Orleans.[10]

On February 8, 1833, Jane and Robert arrived in San Felipe. The town was the headquarters of Austin's operations and contained about thirty single and double log cabins. Williams operated the land office out of his home and Austin's original office had become Whitesides Inn operated by Jonathan Peyton and his wife Angelina, two of Austin's first colonists. They, too, had invested in an eleven-league grant in the upper colony. Possibly Jane stayed at the inn, for she became friends with Angelina and wrote fondly of her twenty years later.[11]

On February 8, 1833, Williams transferred Sawyer's power of attorney for an unlocated eleven-league grant to Doña Jane M. McManus. Sawyer was director of the Arkansas & Texas, the Rio Grande & Texas, and the Colorado & Red River land companies. He also represented the Scot and English empresarios James Grant and John Charles Beales with land grants on the Rio Grande. The transfer document contained the signature of the *alcade*, Luke Lessasieur, and witness statement by Isaac Jones and W. Barret Travis, then a resident of San Felipe. As Travis' surviving diary does not begin until the next August, his impression of the New York woman is unknown.[12]

Jane McManus wrote her declaration of Mexican citizenship in Spanish, claimed the Catholic religion, and received the maximum amount of land a Mexican citizen could possess. The Law of April 6, 1830 stated that only Mexicans could acquire land and the state law set that maximum amount at eleven square leagues. In 1830, the state of *Coahuila y Texas* had issued the grants to finance the state government. Purchasers located the grants on unoccupied land or issued a power of attorney to others to do so. After paying survey and registration fees, land commissioners granted possession to the holder of the grant. Because Austin's and Williams' new colony of less than 100 families had no land commissioner, the nearest *alcade* certified documents. McManus probably paid Sawyer $2,000 for the grant because a week earlier, Robert McAlpin "Three Legged Willie" Williamson quoted that amount to his client, Edward Hanrick, director of the Alabama Land Company in Montgomery. Williamson informed Hanrick that only four of the large grants remained unlocated.[13]

The grant McManus obtained from Sawyer was originally to Perfecto Valdez by the state of *Coahuila y Texas* on July 13, 1830. On July 29, Valdez transferred his power of attorney to file the land claim to Samuel Bangs and Isaac Donoho. Bangs was an associate of the abolitionist Lundy, and Donoho was a Santa Fe trader. Sawyer had acquired the grant two months before transferring it to McManus. Field notes in the Spanish Collection of the Texas General Land Office show that on May 1, 1833, William Moore surveyed the grant specifically for Mrs. Jane McManus on the left bank of the Brazos River slightly above the Waco Indian Village and across from the mouth of the Bosque River and the limestone cliffs of the Comanche Plateau. William McLane, William Taylor, and another assistant witnessed the survey notes. Williams billed McManus $150 for the survey on August 31, 1833. Today, the 49,000 acres extend from Waco's Cameron Park to the vicinity of Elm Mott and along both sides of Interstate 35.[14]

McManus possibly visited the Waco area. Although buyers of eleven-league grants did not normally do so, Williams said that some did. At the time, settlements existed the 200 miles up the Brazos from San Felipe to the Waco Indian village. Above Austin's headquarters lay Groce's Landing at the Coushatta Indian crossing. Next, Andrew Robinson had a ferry near the mouth of the Navasota River on the Spanish La Bahia Road. Farther upstream, a trading post identified the abandoned Mexican Fort Tenoxtitlán at the crossing of the Old San Antonio Road. At the falls of the Brazos and the head of navigation, Francis Smith had a trading post where the Comanche Trail ran eastward to Nacogdoches. Another twenty-odd miles upriver by horseback was a Cherokee settlement about four miles below what remained of the Waco Village. In 1829, mixed-blood Cherokee farmers from Tennessee, the most famous of whom was Jesse Chisolm, killed most of the Waco and Tehuacano Indians after a raid on their livestock. The Cherokees and their twelve associated tribes from east of the Mississippi—Creek, Kichai, Shawnee, Delaware, Kickapoo, Choctaw, Caddo, Seminole, Biloxi, Alabama, and Coushatta—had settled along the Red, Neches, and Sabine rivers. Perhaps Mrs. McManus, described as dark and a Spanish-looking woman, had planned to settle her extended family amidst the Indians all along, a possibility that would explain Burr's comparing her venture to that of Jemima Wilkinson in western New York.[15]

Williams created a power of attorney for Robert to act in his sister's absence. The siblings were to share the grant and the headrights due them under Mexican law as settlers. McManus then began surveying with John Austin along the Trinity River, and Jane returned to New Orleans. By May 20, 1833, she was in New York, where she entered the expenses of a Florida moss gathering expedition in Dey's account ledger.[16]

Because of fraud and counterfeit eleven-league grants, on September 21, 1833, McManus took her copy of the Perfecto Valdez Grant to the Mexican vice-consul in New York, where August Radcliff certified the grant to be true and valid. McManus then began indenturing German immigrants for twelve dollars per year for two years of service in return for passage to Texas. The presence of these particular German immigrants cannot be explained, but in general, Germans came to America at this time because of high unemployment, bad harvests, marginal-sized farms, and a romantic vision of America after the failed European republican revolutions of 1830.[17]

Most Germans entering New Orleans eventually settled in Missouri, but a few trickled into Texas. Germans had migrated to Texas since 1821, and by 1826, more than 200 residents had German surnames. Fifteen thousand Germans came to the United States in 1831. That year, the Galveston Bay Company had one shipload of settlers turned away by Mexican customs officials because the ship had disembarked from New York and violated the ban on settlement from the United States. Some Germans camped near Anahuac, where the Mexican Commander Juan Davis Bradburn allowed them garden plots within the military reserve. On Mill Creek, Germans had a colony, later named Industry, where they raised tobacco and manufactured cigars. F. W. Grasmeyer operated a general store in Matagorda with Jane's future husband, William Leslie Cazneau, then a Boston cotton buyer. Germans also settled in the Frelsburg community on Cummins Creek. Newspapers in Germany advertised Texas land for sale and de Zavala promoted migration from Europe, while José Antonio Mexia directed Germans to Texas from Matamoros. In June 1833, Johann von Racknitz sailed from Le Havre with 200 Germans to settle an eight-league grant on the Colorado River near Bastrop. Although organized with precision, the colony failed because of cholera and a lack of funds for supplies and transit inland.[18]

Late in September 1833, Mrs. McManus chartered a vessel in New York to transport her German indentures and supplies to Texas. Charles Sayre, also bringing Germans, was to share the cost of the ship, but delayed, he withdrew his freight and passengers. In panic, Mrs. McManus wrote Burr for an additional $250 and pleaded, "I cannot go home, you are aware it drained their means to pay for the land." Contrary to Mrs. Burr's later allegations, Jane did not receive funds from Burr. She returned home to Troy, and on October 2, 1833, deeded 500 acres of an unlocated eleven-league grant to Justus Morton for $250. Morton was grand commander of the New York Commandry of Knights Templar and a fraternal brother of her father. Although the land was not hers to deed, Morton had a legal-looking instrument he eventually sold and that later appeared in Matagorda County deed records.[19]

In November 1833, Jane, her brother Robert, and their father, Judge William McManus, an undisclosed number of indentures, auctioneers Logan and C. H. Vandeveer, and unidentified settlers from Kentucky, arrived in Matagorda. Elias Wightman and William Selkirk had established the town in 1829 with fifty-two families from New York and New England. Because of a shortage of timber and poor anchorage, the town had grown little since its founding.[20]

Although Mrs. McManus left no memoirs, Mrs. Annie Fisher Harris described her arrival in Matagorda few months earlier. The harbor was not deep enough for ships, so small boats called lighters transported freight and passengers to and from the deep water to the landing on the Colorado River. A seven-mile logjam blocked the river's mouth and created a giant marsh. The pilgrims walked two miles into town along a path newly cut through the six-foot tall marsh grass from which the town derived its Spanish name—a place of reeds. While some settlers lived in sheds, tents, or in the open, the Fishers first lived in a house with no floor and later shared a room with Judge McManus and his daughter, Jane, at Grasmeyer's store. Harris described Jane as a "woman adventuress" who was "young and handsome," with letters from important people, and she was "useful and agreeable." Karankawa Indians still lived less than a mile from town, and when the women came to trade, they camped beneath Grasmeyer's store built on stilts. The Indians had Spanish names, yet they wore only animal skin skirts and wreaths of leaves around their necks. During the full moon, Matagorda residents could hear the Indians singing, and as they danced and beat their drums, coyotes howled in the distance.[21]

The indentures broke their contracts with Mrs. McManus and refused to go further inland. Either they were frightened by the story of Josiah Wilbarger, the local schoolteacher who was scalped by Indians upriver and lived to tell of it, or word spread that Robertson had gained control of the upper colony and refused to honor Williams' transactions. Perhaps the Germans learned they could have land by filing a claim at the land office.[22]

While in Texas, Judge McManus acted as Swartwout's agent. Burr's former secretary was customs inspector for the Port of New York, held shares in the Galveston Bay & Texas Land Company, and in those companies under Sawyer's direction—the Arkansas & Texas, the Rio Grande & Texas, and Colorado & Red River land companies. Presumably, Judge McManus handled the preliminaries for development of another Swartwout interest, the New Washington Association. First discussed in 1829, the project was the work of Dr. Thomas Cooley, a social architect, and John R. Bartlett, later founder of the American Ethnological Society and United States Boundary Commissioner. The reformers visited Matagorda in 1833 and then selected the 1,600-acre site of Clopper's Point on Galveston Bay for a social experiment to blend Europeans and free blacks in an agricultural and a commercial venture. The directors were Lorenzo de Zavala, John P. Austin, James Treat, Stephen Sicard, James Watson Webb, editor of the New York *Courier & Enquirer*, and Mordecai Noah, editor of the New York *Star*. Joseph L. Joseph was a financier, and the general manager was James Morgan. The latter provisioned a store at Anahuac for settlers in the area of the Galveston Bay Company where James Prentiss purchased scrip and established the Union and Trinity land companies. Impressed with Judge McManus, the City of Matagorda deeded him twelve acres of city lots on March 31, 1834, in exchange for his building a sawmill which would aid in development. In April 1834, Jane and her father returned to New York, where she again entered expenses in Dey's ledgers.[23]

Because of New York's liberal laws, the black population had grown by sixty-five percent in a decade. In 1830, New York had 44,870, or one-third of the black population of the northern states. Until 1848, when a Free Soil-controlled legislature revised the law, New York blacks with $250 in property could vote, and Whigs labeled them "Jackson whites" because they voted Democratic. While the American Colonization Society encouraged free blacks to migrate to Liberia and create a black republic, British abolitionist George Thompson, funded by the London-based World Anti-Slavery Society, toured the United States and declared the American Colonial Society "the enemy of the people of color." Thompson and William Lloyd Garrison encouraged free blacks to claim the United States as the country of their birth. In Catholic countries and Europe, no stigma attached to being black, thus, the New Washington venture was a viable solution to relocate New York's growing population of unskilled blacks and Europeans.[24]

Meanwhile, relations between the Mexican government and the Texans deteriorated. Since January 1834, Stephen F. Austin had been in prison in Mexico City because he advised Texas officials to form a government independent of Coahuila. Austin remained caught in the power struggle between centralists who wanted Texas controlled from Mexico City and federalists in Saltillo who wanted Texas to be a part of Coahuila. By March 1834, the legislature of Coahuila y Texas moved from Saltillo because of its centralist leanings to federalist Monclova and sold an additional 400 unlocated, eleven-league grants to arm a state militia.

John T. Mason, agent for the Galveston Bay & Texas Land Company, purchased all 400 grants. In Mexico City, Anthony Butler botched plans Pres. Andrew Jackson had for the United States to buy Texas by not reading his instructions until he reached Mexico City. Meanwhile, Santa Anna, who had assumed control of the government, ordered new state elections, named his brother-in-law, Martin Perfecto Cós, commander-general of the Mexican army, closed Congress, and suspended all liberal laws passed by his predecessor, Valentíne Goméz Farías.[25]

In November 1834, Jane and Robert McManus planned to return to Texas, but their father was in poor health, and on January 18, 1835, William McManus died of a heart attack. Word quickly spread of his death, and by the end of January, Swartwout wrote the East Texas surveyor, José María Carvajal, that Col. Frost Thorn of Nacogdoches had assumed McManus's former duties.[26]

Unable to develop the grant near the Waco Indian village because of the Robertson and Williams dispute over settlement rights, Jane McManus applied to Williams for eight leagues of land near Matagorda. It was then that the Texas Revolution began and Mrs. McManus returned to New York, where she found a scandal involving the seventy-six-year-old Burr. In 1834, Burr's wife of less than a year filed for divorce to regain control of her remaining finances that he had not spent on Texas land speculations. Mrs. Burr named Jane McManus in the divorce Bill of Complaint as having had an affair with Burr, and her maid gave testimony as to explicit sex acts she had witnessed.[27]

In October, Texans held a Consultation and called for the restoration of the Mexican Constitution of 1824. Delegates ordered the land offices closed because of confusion and arguments over land claims that distracted participants. During Williams' absences to New Orleans and elsewhere, Gail Borden, Jr., the son of the local blacksmith, maintained the land records, but primarily coordinated the Texan's committees of correspondence. Thus, many claims in the San Felipe land office were unfinished. In Nacogdoches, George Nixon registered claims beyond the closing date. In all, 1,400 claims were "unfinished," including the land and headright claims of Jane McManus.[28]

McManus had more difficulties than unfinished land grants and the Burr divorce scandal. Williams had altered the land office copy of her Valdez Grant. He had erased Perfecto Valdez on the first page and inserted Rafael de Aguirre. Later in court, Williams claimed that Perfecto Valdez was inserted in error on subsequent pages, but, as Gaylon Greaser, translator of Spanish documents in the General Land Office explained, mistakes were never erased but lined through and explained at the end of documents similar to endnotes. The best explanation is that Williams needed four grants for Handrick's Alabama Land Company in April 1833, when the speculators came to inspect the land for which they had made a deposit in the form of drafts that Williams had already cashed. With the three grants of Tomás de la Vega, Raphael de Aguirre, and José Maria Aguirre still unlocated and with that of Mrs. McManus altered as the second Rafael de Aguirre grant, Williams had four grants for the Alabamians. Asa Hoxey located the altered grant on the San Gabriel River in present Williamson County.[29]

While her brother became a hero of the Texas Revolution, Jane traded land claims for room and board and legal fees for a perjury suit against Mrs. Burr's maid. In December 1837, Jane returned to Texas and registered her land claims. The Texas government refused to honor eleven-league grants because Texans thought the 1,100 grants issued by the Monclova legislature in 1834 and 1835 caused Santa Anna's march north. The Constitution of the Republic denied the grants purchased by Mason as agent of the Galveston Bay & Texas Land Company. Furthermore, only Texas residents could own land; claims were to be registered, and conflicts settled in local courts.[30]

In January 1838, Jane registered the Waco, Matagorda, and headright claims that totaled 83,272 acres. The Texas Land Board and Matagorda County Commissioners agreed that her claims were valid, but others had claimed the same land. By late November, rumors of the Burr scandal spread to Matagorda and Jane's rivals used the gossip to their advantage. A Mississippi faction with claims to her Matagorda land refused her entry to a public ball, asserting she was unfit for respectable society. The incident almost caused a duel when Ira R. Lewis, William Cazneau, and Charles DeMorse, later editor of the Clarksville *Northern Standard*, defended Jane's honor and challenged the adversaries to a duel. The newspaper reported that a decision made at a public meeting determined the circumstance did not merit such drastic action. In January 1839, McManus sold her father's city lots and returned to New York.[31]

To earn a living for herself and her son, McManus, again used her married name, Storm, and became a journalist. She wrote for the New York *Tribune*, the New York *Sun*, and anonymously for the *United States Magazine & Democratic Review*. She returned to Texas on land business in the 1840s and transferred one-half of her headright claim to Swartwout for his payment of her legal debts. Thomas J. Chambers received the other half for his legal assistance in getting the claim recognized. According to Swartwout and James Morgan, Jane could have gotten all her land had she only married Anthony Butler, the former minister to

Mexico who lived in Washington County, or an unnamed wealthy New Orleans gentleman.[32]

McManus would not settle in Texas but did write on behalf of Texas for the New York press. Textual analysis indicates she wrote the expansionist materials in the *Sun* and on manifest destiny attributed to John L. O'Sullivan in the *Democratic Review* that convinced New Yorkers to vote for James K. Polk and Texas annexation. Perhaps for her service to Texas, Adolphus Sterne deeded Jane McManus 1,283 acres of land on Carrizo Creek. She traveled to Mexico on diplomatic missions during the Mexican War and was involved in the 1849 Narciso Lopez filibuster activities that resulted in indictments of New Yorkers. It was then that Jane left New York and married Texas border trader William Cazneau. She wrote of her experiences as *Eagle Pass: or Life on the Border* (1852). With the assistance of Secretary of State William L. Marcy, she secured a diplomatic post for William Cazneau in the Dominican Republic, and the Cazneaus spent the remainder of their lives in the Caribbean. Throughout her career, as Cora Montgomery, Jane promoted territorial and commercial expansion into Texas, Mexico, the Caribbean, and Central America. She published more than a hundred signed newspaper columns in six metropolitan newspapers, more than twenty articles in three national journals, fifteen or more books and pamphlets, and edited five or more newspapers and journals. She was in the process of returning to Texas to continue her land claim battles but died at sea in 1878 when the *Emily B. Souder* came apart in heavy seas and sank near Bermuda.[33]

NOTES

1. At the time of this submission, Linda S. Hudson was adjunct professor of American history at Texas Christian University. In 2001, her biography of Cazneau, *Mistress of Manifest Destiny*, was published by the Texas State Historical Association.

2. Dey Records, Yale, box 2, fol. 28, box 4, fols. 80-82, 88, 90.

3. Dey Records, box 4, fol. 85.

4. Depositions, Bill of Complaint, Jumel Papers, NYHS; Gustavus Myers, *The History of Tammany Hall* (New York, 1917), p. 53; *Texas und Einlandung zu einer vortheilhaften Unsiedelung daselbt* (Stuttgart, 1835), Dey Records, Yale, box 4, fol. 90.

5. Sheridan, *McManus*, p. 2; *Las Siete Partidas*, Bexar Archives, San Antonio, vol. 17, p. 1; Col. Burr to J.M. McManus, November 17, 1832, Aaron Burr Papers, New York Historical Society, New York, New York, hereinafter cited as Burr Papers, NYHS; Robert P. St. John, "Jemima Wilkinson," *Quarterly Journal of the New York Historical Association*, 11 (April 1930), p. 169.

6. Aaron Burr to Judge Workman, November 16, 1832, Burr Papers, NYHS; Thomas Perkins Abernethy, *The Burr Conspiracy* (Glouchester, Massachusetts, 1968), pp. 16-25, 73-74, 167-168, 240, 268.

7. Burr to Workman, November 16, 1832, Burr Papers, NYHS.

8. Margaret Henson, *Samuel May Williams: Early Texas Entrepreneur* (College Station, 1976), pp. 53-54, hereinafter cited as Henson, *Williams*; Malcolm McLean, comp. and ed., *Papers Concerning Robertson's Colony in Texas*, 19 vols. (Arlington, 1980), VII, 49, hereinafter cited as McLean, comp., *Robertson's Colony*; Judith N. McArthur, "Myth, Reality, and Anomaly: The Complex World of Rebecca Haggerty," *East Texas Historical Journal* (Fall 1986), p. 23.

9. Charles D. Sayre to S. M. Williams, January 22, February 3, 1833, SMW Papers; Henson, *Bradburn*, p. 83.

10. Henson, *Williams*, pp. 16-17, 23-25; J. M. Storm to M. B. Lamar, October 1845, No. 2195, Papers of Mirabeau Buonaparte Lamar, Archives and Records Division, Texas State Library, Austin; Mrs. William L. Cazneau, *Eagle Pass, or Life on the Border* (New York, 1852; Austin, 1966), p. 15.

11. "Perfecto Valdez," Spanish Collection, Archives and Records Division, Texas General Land Office, Austin, box 23, fol. 23, hereinafter cited as Spanish Collection, GLO.; Andreas V. Reichstein, *Rise of the Lone Star: The Making of Texas* (College Station, 1989), p. 109, hereinafter cited as Reichstein, *Lone Star*; Robert E. Davis, ed., *The Diary of William Barret Travis*, August 30, 1833 to June 26, 1834 (Waco, 1966), p. 36.

12. Jane Cazneau Vertical File, Center For American History, University of Texas at Austin, hereinafter cited as Cazneau File, CAH.; McLean, comp., *Robertson's Colony*, VII, pp. 44-49.

13. Field Notes, box X, p. 292, box 23, fol. 23, Spanish Collection, GLO; McLean, *Robertson's Colony*, VII, pp. 47, 49, 525; A. Ray Stephens and William M. Holmes, *Historical Atlas of Texas* (Norman, 1989), No. 22, "Empresario Grants," hereinafter cited as Stephens, Atlas; LeRoy P. Graf, "Colonizing Projects in Texas South of the Nueces, 1820-1845," *Southwestern Historical Quarterly*, 50 (April 1947), p. 440; Merton L. Dillon, *Benjamin Lundy and the Struggle for Negro Freedom* (Urbana, 1966), pp. 224-5.

14. James Armstrong, *Some Facts on the Eleven League Controversy* (Austin, 1859), pp. 5, 11, 13, hereinafter cited as Armstrong, *Eleven-League*; Stephens, *Atlas*, no. 24 "Texas in 1835"; Ray Miller, *Texas Forts: A History and Guide* (Houston, 1985), p. 208; McLean, comp., *Robertson's Colony*, VII, p. 355; Betty Dooley Awbrey and Claude Dooley, *Why Stop? A Guide to Texas Historical Markers*, 3rd Ed., (Houston, 1992), pp. 295, 299; Patricia Ward Wallace, *Waco Texas Crossroads* (Woodland Hills, California, 1983), p. 15; John Henry Brown, *Pioneers of Texas* (Austin, 1880; Greenville, 1978), pp. 12, 25, 121, hereinafter cited as Brown, *Pioneers*; s.v. "Jemima Wilkinson," Allen Johnson, ed., *Dictionary of American Biography* (New York, 1936).

15. "Perfecto Valdez," Spanish Collection, GLO; Samuel Sawyer to John Austin, July 14, 1833, SMW Papers; "Account Book, 1828-1834," ser. 4, box 6, fol. 93, p. 258-259, Dey Records, Yale.

16. "Perfecto Valdez," Spanish Collection, GLO; Mack Walker, *Germany and the Emigration 1816-1885* (Cambridge, 1964), pp. 42-50, 58-68, hereinafter cited as Walker, *German Emigration*; J. McManus to Col. Burr, n.d. Jumel Papers, NYHS.

17. Mattie Austin Hatcher, *The Opening of Texas to Foreign Settlement 1801-1821* (Austin, 1927; Philadelphia, 1976), pp. 273-274; Don H. Biggers, *German Pioneers in Texas* (Fredericksburg, 1925), pp. 6-12; Walker, *German Emigration*, pp. 42-50, 58, 62-67; Brister, "von Racknitz," pp. 56-61.

18. McManus to Burr, n. d., Jumel Papers, NYHS; Jane McManus to Justus Morton, $250, October 2, 1833, Matagorda County Deed Records, Bay City, Book A, pp. 92-93.

19. R. O. W. McManus to S. Rhodes Fisher, June 22, 1885, John Herndon James Papers, 1812-1938, Daughters of the Republic of Texas Library At the Alamo, San Antonio, hereinafter cited as James Papers, DRT; Matagorda County Historical Commission, *Historic Matagorda County*, 2 vols. (Houston, 1986), vol. 1, p. 33; Brown, *Pioneers*, pp. 23-25; Gilbert Giddings Benjamin, *Germans In Texas* (Philadelphia: Report No. 7, German American Annuals, 1909), pp. 15-22. George Erath and the Biegel, Dietrich, and Ehllinger families came in 1833.

20. Ethel Mary Franklin, ed., "Memories of Mrs. Annie P. Harris," *Southwestern Historical Quarterly*, 40 (January 1937), pp 231-234, 239, hereinafter cited as Franklin, ed., "Annie Harris,"; Lorraine Bruce Jeter, *Matagorda Early History* (Baltimore, 1974), p. 18; William Goetzmann, *Army Exploration in the West, 1803-1863* (New Haven, 1959; Austin, 1991), p. 23, hereinafter cited as Goetzmann, *Exploration*.; City of Matagorda, *Constitution*, March 24, 1834.

21. Franklin, ed., "Annie Harris," p. 239; Henson, *Williams*, pp. 57-60.

22. Sheridan, *McManus*, pp. 35-36; A. B. J. Hammell, *The Empressario: Don Martin DeLeon* (Waco, 1973), p. 163, hereinafter cited as Hammell, *DeLeon*; Reichstein, *Lone Star*, pp. 107-109; "James Prentiss," NHT 5, 326; Keith Guthrie, *Texas Forgotten Ports*, 3 vols. (Austin, 1995), 3, pp. 41-44; Goetzmann, *Exploration*, p. 168; "Account Book," box 4, fol. 85, Dey Records, Yale; Matagorda, *Constitution*, March 24, 1834; Passenger Lists of Vessels Arriving at New Orleans, 1820-1902, Reel #12, August 5, 1833-May 1835, M257 National Archives, Washington, D.C.

23. J. E. B. DeBow, ed., *Statistical View of the United States ... Being a Compendium of the Seventh Census* . . . (Washington, 1854) 4, p. ix; Eric Foner, "Politics and Prejudice: The Free Soil Party and the Negro, 1849-1852," *Journal of Negro History*, 50 (Oct. 1965), p. 239; William Lloyd Garrison, *Lectures of George Thompson: History of His Connection with the Anti-Slavery Cause in England* (Boston, 1836), pp. xix, xxvi, 179-180; Petition of G. L. Thompson, September 5, 1829, Duff Green Papers, National Archives, Washington, D.C.; Franklin, ed., "Annie Harris," pp. 238, 245.

24. Margaret Swett Henson, *Lorenzo de Zavala* (Fort Worth, 1996), pp. 72-75; Gerald D. Saxon, "Anthony Butler: A Flawed Diplomat," *East Texas Historical Journal* (Spring 1986), pp 5-8.

25. Sheridan, *McManus*, pp. 2, 5; Troy *Budget* January 30, 1835; Hammell, *DeLeon*, p. 163.

26. J. M. McManus to S. M. Williams, June 19, 1835, SMW Papers; Villame Williams, ed., *Stephen F. Austin Register of Families* (Baltimore, 1984), Appendix, R-2, March 17, 1835; Depositions, Jumel Papers, NYHS.

27. Margaret Swett Henson and Deolece Parmelee, *The Cartwrights of San Augustine* (Austin, 1993), p. 92; Henson, *Williams*, p. 76; "Spanish and Mexican Records in the General Land Office," Indices, GLO.

28. McLean, comp., *Robertson's Colony*, VII, p. 49; Samuel M. Williams to Francis W. Johnson, December 1, 1832, SMW Papers; Robert M. Williamson to Asa Hoxey, February, 2, April, 13, 15, August 26, 1833, Hoxey to Edward Hanrick, November 6, 27, 1833, Edward Hanrick Papers, Center for American History, University of Texas, Austin, hereinafter cited as Hanrick Papers, CAH; Armstrong, *Eleven-League*, pp. 5, 11, 13.

29. Jane M. McManus to Joseph D. Beers, October 29, 1835, SMW Papers; Jane Cazneau File, CAH; Republic of Texas Constitution, General Provisions, Section 10.

30. Armstrong, *Eleven-League*, pp. 1-11; Divorce Proceedings, box 1, fol. 13, 5, Jumel Papers, NYHS.; William Cary Duncan, *The Amazing Madame Jumel* (New York, 1935), pp. 4, 129-131, 226, 259, 264-266; Samuel H. Wandell and Meade Minnigerode, *Aaron Burr, A Biography Compiled from rare, and in many cases unpublished sources* (New York, 1925), p. 328; Spanish Collection, GLO, box 23, fol. 23; Gifford White, "Clerks Reports for the Board of Land Commissioners of Matagorda County, issued from Jan. 1 to Mar. 1, 1838," *First Settlers of Matagorda County, Texas* (Austin, 1986), pp. 14, 16, 20, 27; Jane M. McManus to J. T. Belknap, December 31, 1839, 12 lots, Matagorda County Deed Records, 1837-1872, Book B, p. 347, Matagorda County Court House, Bay City.

31. Marion Tinling, *Women Remembered: A Guide to Landmarks of Women's History in the United States* (New York, 1986), p. 273; The only known marker to Cazneau is in Matagorda.; Gifford White, ed., *The 1840 Census of the Republic of Texas* (Austin, 1966), 103; R. O. W. McManus, GLO, Claims fols. 1-000231 09; 1-000297 10; 1-001397 01; B-000195 08; B-001600 01; C-005593 00. He is buried in the Texas

State Cemetery, Austin; James Morgan to Samuel Swartwout, February 1, 1838, Swartwout to Morgan, May 6, 1838, Morgan to Swartwout, June 10, 1838, James Morgan Papers, Texas Collection, Rosenberg Library, Galveston; "The Ups and downs of an Eccentric Inventor," Troy *Daily Press* January 26, 1891; "Estate of Jane M. Cazneau, Probate Proceedings," in *Abstract of Title to Antonio Rivas Grant in Maverick County, Texas* (San Antonio, 1938), p. 15; J. Maria McManus to Sam Houston, April 20, 1840, Sam Houston Papers, Catholic Archives, Austin; Asa P. Ufford to Edward Hanrick, October 25, 1854, Hanrick Papers, CAH, Austin; Armstrong, *Eleven-League*, 13-16. The Alabama planters went bankrupt in 1837. Hoxey's land reverted to Hanrick, who was imprisoned for debt in Baltimore. The land reverted to the Bank of the United States then to Asa and Joseph Ufford. The Uffords sued for possession in Williamson County courts where, in the 1850s, the Williams fraud was discovered. The McManus attorney was the Fisher baby who lived with the McManus family at Cazneau's store in Matagorda. R. O. W. McManus to S. Rhodes Fisher, June 1885, James Papers, DRT-Alamo.

32. Julius Pratt, "The Origins of 'Manifest Destiny'," *American Historical Review*, 32 (July 1927), pp. 795-798. In 1927, Pratt traced the first use of the term "manifest destiny" to the anonymous article, "Annexation," in the July-August 1845 issue of the *United States Magazine and Democratic Review*. Pratt assumed that editor, John L. O'Sullivan, wrote the article.; Linda Sybert Hudson, "Jane McManus Storm Cazneau: A Biography," Ph.D. dissertation, University of North Texas, 1999, Appendix B, "Grammatical Analysis." Textual analysis of articles signed by Cazneau, O'Sullivan, and the anonymous "Annexation"showed that her writing style had an overall 79.6 percent similarity to the anonymous article, whereas O'Sullivan displayed a 41.5 percent similarity. Grammatical errors were one hundred percent similar to Cazneau's with O'Sullivan having none.; Harriet Smither, ed., "The Diary of Adolphus Sterne," *Southwestern Historical Quarterly*, 38 (July 1934), pp. 58, 149, 153.

Writing Coffee Table History without Getting Verklempt: Fort Worth and the New Frontier

Ty Cashion

Thanks for the introduction. As a native son, born in Kilgore, I am very humbled to have served as an officer of the East Texas Historical Association. I worked in business ten years before taking the plunge into TCU's Ph.D. program. If I were a better businessman, I probably would not be here now. I was an economist for a utilities company that in Texas, at least, served mostly rural areas. During that time, I traveled the state and read a lot about all the places I was visiting. So, in that respect, I knew Archie McDonald a long time before I ever met him. There are others here in the room who I knew by your works as well. So, I have to pinch myself sometimes when I think that I know so many of you and even count you among my friends.

I am also a fourth-generation Texan, and my momma's people came here from Bohemia and Moravia in the 1840s. Now, the Bohemian in me is starting to bubble up; I'm getting all *verklempt*. Let me give you a topic: "The Texas Revolution did not really involve Texans, nor was it truly a revolution in the classic sense." Discuss amongst yourselves. . . . . OK, I'm better.

Not long after Archie and Mark Barringer told me I had better submit a title if I wanted to serve out my term as president, I started putting something together that I thought might be instructional as well as entertaining. Then, a funny thing happened that changed what I was going to say. And once again, just a few weeks ago, another funny thing happened. All of this is coffee-table-history related. Actually, neither one of them were ha-ha funny; more like a visceral jolt. Let me tell you about the first funny and then I'll close with the second one and share some interesting examples.

My project was a coffee table history of Fort Worth. I have completed the text, and the photo editing is almost done. What I had envisioned was standing up here saying that just because a book has got a lot of pictures in it does not mean it cannot rest on primary sources and have an interpretation that still says something good about the subject. Most of you know how little we make on books. I always get a good chuckle out of my buddies from the old days, when they ask, "What are you going to do with all the money from that book?" And I tell them, "Aw, I'll probably take [wife] Peggy and [son] Sam out to dinner." They laugh. Then, I laugh at them for thinking that I am only kidding! In fact, I have a theory—the only folks making money off writing books are the ones whose names are bigger than the title of the book.

So, when this publisher who produces community histories calls waving some cash in my direction, I told him I was already working on another project; thanks, but no thanks. Then, I started thinking, "You know, I sure could use that money; I know the VISA card folks would like to have some of it." Jim Olson told me, "Heck, yeah. I could do something like that in a few weeks." Well, let me tell you a little secret about Jim Olson. (Sometimes I think he makes sure he tells me it is a secret, just knowing that I will get the word out more quickly!) He once wrote a 250-page reader on civil rights over a Christmas break and still had time to go shopping for the dozens of kids and grandkids he has.

Well, here it is two years later, and it is not looking like mine will be a stocking stuffer under anybody's Christmas tree this year. In fact, I am afraid to calculate how much money I made if you break it down by the hour and deduct the gas and mileage from all those trips to Fort Worth. The way the publisher was going to make money was by selling community profiles, which he would stick in the back half of the book. He had television newsman Ron Stone doing one for Houston, and another local notable, Mike Ward, doing one for Austin.

This past summer, I had some trouble getting the guy to return my calls, so I contacted the other authors to see if it was just me, or what's going on? To make a long story short, they had finished their books more than a year ago, but the guy was still selling pages, and they were wondering if they would ever see them in print. Boy, talk about a sinking feeling. Let me put this on record. I truly believe the publisher had good intentions, and he just got a little overwhelmed with so many irons in the fire. After checking around, I learned that he had not started working on Fort Worth yet, so I began looking for a back door to that contract. Little did I know that he was out in California trying to do the same thing. So, I'm hoping it all works out. I told him to keep the money he owed me and just give me back that copyright. Boy, he was all over that like a pack of feral hogs on the circus fat man!

Like most of the other stuff I write, it will probably cost me more than I make, but at least it is with a good university press, and there will not be any pages in the back. [Editor's note: Eventually, the original company published Cashion's Fort Worth book.] Not that that is bad, but when you spend a couple of years on something, you would rather have the scholarship than the money. Did I tell you if I were a better businessman, I wouldn't be here? Well, it was my goal to stand up here and tell you something instructional. So, here it is: "A Ph.D. does not necessarily make you any smarter—and I prove it every day!"

Seriously, I do have one thing instructional to say: Don't ever illustrate a book! Man, it took me longer to shag pictures, get releases, arrange for prints, and all that, than it did to do the research and writing. At least Carol Roarke, the author of several eloquent and well-illustrated books, was delighted to hear me say that! When I called her to complain about it, she kept laughing so hard that we never got down to a serious conversation.

That leads me to the other funny. Olson and I were at a gathering, and he told me, "The president wants to see you and me next Monday." My heart almost exploded! Why the heck would the president want to see me? This can't be good. Well, it was, but it wasn't. He asked me to write a coffee table history to commemorate the 125th anniversary of Sam Houston State University. I said: "Man, I am just as flattered as I can be. When do you want it?" "JUNE" he says. WHEW! When I got home, I had one of those Sally Field moments when I told my wife: "Peg, they like me, they really like me!" Without batting an eye, she reached over and tapped me on the forehead and said, "No they don't; none of *them* wanted to do it!" The very next day, I was at the annual football parents' luncheon, and I told our president what my wife had said. He looked at me, and then he cut a look at his wife and said, "She does that to me all the time, too."

In the few minutes I have left, let me share with you a sampling of what will go into that coffee table book on Fort Worth. Just because it is coffee table history, does not mean you cannot go out and dig up primary source information, have an interpretation, or avoid the things that do not exactly reflect well on your subject—in my case, Fort Worth. You have to know who your reading audience is. There is a problem with including everything; you have to be selective. Where I had a word count that was exhausted, I used illustrations to cover some of the material history. For example, early on, I included an 1890 panoramic image of the city from the Board of Trade Building at Houston and West Seventh with the recently completed Texas Spring Palace and the beginning construction of St. Patrick's Catholic Church in view.

When I complained to Jim Olson about not having enough space to write everything, he told me something that was extremely valuable: "Nobody wants to read a 500-page coffee table history. Keep it short and sweet, kind of like an after-dinner address!" You avoid some things. Take the actions of individuals who did bad things, such as the oil millionaire who financed a racist campaign (see George Green's book). It involved the city in a larger arena, but it did not affect Fort Worth directly. So, what do you do? I chose to ignore it. Of course, the bad things can make the big picture more meaningful and interesting. The two murder trials of millionaire T. Cullen Davis were major events in Fort Worth in 1976 and 1977. Flamboyant defense attorney Richard "Racehorse" Haynes and Davis, his smiling and chatty defendant, provided quite interesting photographs.

Let me mention a few other images that demonstrate the arc of Fort Worth history as I envisioned it for the book. The city's early public transportation system depended on sometimes not so dependable mule-drawn streetcars, which were replaced by cars of the Northern Texas Traction Company and later the Trinity Railway Express. I was able to find images of these systems and they added much to the attraction of the text.

Of course, pictures show the downside of history as well. Hooded Klansmen on the march and a formal photograph of the Rev. J. Frank Norris, an outspoken Klan supporter, are examples, as is a photo of white teenagers in 1956 protesting attempts to integrate the Riverside neighborhood. Some of these challenges have been overcome, though none completely.

As far as presidential addresses go, I hope this has accomplished my intentions—that is, to provide you with something you might find edifying as well as interesting. Let me close by saying that I will always be grateful to all of you for the warmth and good cheer you have extended to me during my term as president of the East Texas Historical Association. There have been some truly outstanding people who have preceded me, and no doubt there will be many more to follow. It has been a privilege to serve. With a healthy measure of Christian humility, let me express appreciation for the opportunities this association extended to me professionally. But more than that—way more than that—please know that the many friendships this organization has presented mean so much more. Thank you and God bless.

The Civil Rights Bill of 1964: One Small Town's Contribution

Gail Beil

In 1982, journalist Bill Moyers came home to film *Marshall Texas/Marshall Texas,* an Emmy Award-winning documentary about his hometown. Moyers choose the double title to make a point. Like most southern towns of his youth, Marshall was two separate communities, one black and one white. Although Moyers did not mention it at the time, he and James Farmer, another Marshallite who appeared on his television program, had a great deal to do with changing that condition, sharing the optimistic goal of making those two communities truly one. The evolution began with the passage of Pres. Lyndon Johnson's Civil Rights Act of 1964.

Farmer and Moyers each had a major role in the 1964 legislation. Farmer dramatically demonstrated the need for change and Moyers played an intimate role in the passage of the bill itself, but they were not the only Marshallites who had a part in getting the measure to the president's desk; the others were first lady, Lady Bird Johnson, and the Johnson family cook, Zephyr Wright. The impact of the legislation on Marshall, and by implication the rest of the South, was summed up in one of the interviews in Moyers' 1983 documentary. Asked about the effect of the 1964 Civil Rights Bill, Moyers' senior English teacher, said, "Well, today we lost the Civil War. Up to that time we had always won it."[1]

The segregated churches, movie houses and public schools of Marshall, as well as Wiley College, had an effect on all four—Farmer, Moyers, Johnson and Wright—molding them in ways that would profoundly affect the Civil Rights Act of 1964.

James Leonard Farmer, Jr.

James Leonard Farmer Jr. was born in Marshall on January 12, 1920. His father, J. Leonard Farmer, Texas' first black Ph.D., was a professor of religion and philosophy at Wiley College. Dr. Farmer accepted a teaching job at Rust College in Holly Springs, Mississippi, the next year, and taught at Samuel Huston College in Austin, Texas, after that. The family returned to Marshall in 1934, when the younger Farmer was a senior at Central (later Pemberton) High School and his father was again professor and dean of the college chapel at Wiley College. Young Farmer graduated from Marshall's segregated black high school at age 14, and enrolled at Wiley in 1935. It was there that Farmer came under the tutelage of Melvin B. Tolson, English and speech professor, and long the campus radical. Farmer spoke and wrote of a growing awareness of the injustice of segregation and its codification into law in many cases, an awareness taught him by Tolson, who was his debate coach.[2]

Farmer's student conversations with Tolson, who said Jim Crow was verbally stomped to death and properly buried, were too often followed by trips the next day to the local movie theater, where all African Americans had to sit in the "buzzard's roost"—the balcony. That intellectual schizophrenia, Farmer said, stimulated him to become a catalyst in the effort to end *de jure* segregation. "I decided it out of my contact here with Professor Tolson," Farmer told Moyers in *Marshall Texas/Marshall Texas*. Farmer Jr. received his Masters of Divinity from Howard University School of theology in Washington, DC, but did not follow his father into the Methodist ministry. Instead, he decided ending segregation was to be his calling. Soon after, he organized the Congress of Racial Equality (CORE).

In February 1961, Farmer and CORE burst into the newspaper headlines all over the nation. The Freedom Rides had begun and Farmer was on the front seat of the bus. Two Supreme Court cases motivated Farmer and his fellow CORE participants. The decision in *Irene Moore v. Virginia* in 1946 ruled segregation on interstate travel unconstitutional. The *Boynton v. Virginia* decision in 1960 ruled that segregation was illegal in the facilities themselves if they served interstate travelers.[3] It was the intention of the dozen riders on two buses leaving Washington in May to make their way through the South to New Orleans, testing the restrooms, lunch counters, and water fountains in small towns in Georgia, Alabama, Mississippi and Louisiana along the way. The Kennedys—Attorney General Robert as well as the president—opposed such a potentially violent confrontation, and Martin Luther King had also questioned the wisdom of such a trip, as did Thurgood Marshall and Roy Wilkins. Farmer refused to call off the Freedom Rides, however, even when all the CORE men and women on the two buses had to be hospitalized because of beatings and smoke inhalation they suffered. The Ku Klux Klan torched one of the buses outside Anniston, Alabama, and a mob descended on the other in Birmingham.

Photographs of the burning bus made newspapers from the *New York Times* and the *Washington Post* to the *Marshall News Messenger*. Members of the Student Nonviolent Coordinating Committee (SNCC), as well as CORE, began venturing into Alabama and Mississippi, filling the jails. For three months, Freedom Riders poured into the South and were roughed up and arrested as television cameras rolled and news photographers filled roll after roll of film. When it was over, the press and politicians promoted Farmer as one of the most important figures in the modern civil rights movement, and the treatment of African Americans in the Deep South was the subject of conversation in the halls of Congress as well as the newsrooms of the nation.[4]

Though Farmer agreed that Johnson sincerely wanted the Civil Rights Bill of 1964 to pass, he said the president hated the marches and the demonstrations. Farmer, on the other hand, knew that without them, the impetus to get a bill passed would fade. For this reason, Farmer did not remain an intimate of Johnson for long, as did the other three Marshallites. Early in the Johnson administration, Farmer was often at the White House or the recipient of a telephone call from the president. CORE's agitation for the integration of public accommodations and voting rights led by Farmer, though, kept the issue of civil rights in focus for Johnson and the lawmakers.

Bill Moyers

Born in Hugo, Oklahoma, but reared in Marshall, Moyers graduated with honors from Marshall High School. Just as Farmer had been, Moyers was identified early in his life as precocious. Publisher Millard Cope hired Moyers, then sixteen years old, as a reporter for the *Marshall News Messenger* and assigned him to beats normally reserved for more mature reporters.[5] Moyers attended North Texas University, graduated from the University of Texas, and completed his master's in theology from Southwestern Baptist Seminary in Fort Worth. Just like Farmer, Jr., Moyers elected not to enter the ministry. He received an offer of a teaching position at Baylor University in Waco but turned it down to enter the world of politics.[6]

With the recommendation of Cope, Moyers first worked for Sen. Lyndon Johnson as an undergraduate at North Texas University. He was an important part of the Kennedy-Johnson campaign of 1960 and afterward rewarded with the position of deputy director of the Peace Corps under Kennedy brother-in-law, Sargent Shriver. At the time, he was one of the youngest men ever confirmed by the Senate.[7] He became a special assistant to the president when Johnson moved into the White House in 1963. Moyers' face, with black, horn-rimmed glasses, can be seen behind Johnson's left shoulder on Air Force One as Judge Sarah T. Hughes administered the oath of office to Johnson following the assassination of Pres. John F. Kennedy, November 22, 1963.[8] Writers, particularly reporters and other Johnson staff members during the Johnson era, place Moyers deep in Johnson's inner circle, the only staff member with a good relationship with the Kennedys. Moyers was one of the southern liberals in the administration and a gifted wordsmith. His official title was special assistant, and in that position he coordinated legislation, particularly the civil rights and antipoverty bills, and wrote speeches. Before Moyers left the White House, he also served as press secretary to the president. He eventually departed in 1967 and now rarely discusses those years, especially for publication. He is one of the few who served in the Johnson administration not to write a book about his stint in public service. In the years afterward, Moyers has become an award-winning journalist in print as well as television.[9]

Zephyr Wright

Zephyr Stephens Wright was a student at Wiley College while employed by Lady Bird Johnson, whose husband was then in the U.S. House of Representatives. In an interview in 1974 with Mike Gillette, then oral history director of the Lyndon B. Johnson Library in Austin, Wright said that she, too, had been a student of Melvin B. Tolson. As he had earlier with Farmer, Tolson made Wright see that conditions for African Americans in Marshall and elsewhere were not acceptable. "That was one of the things that I realized later on in life, that this was the beginning of my realizing what segregation was all about. Because I had come up with the idea that this was the way life was going to be and there was nothing I could do about it," Wright said in the 1974 interview. "But after I went to school there [at Wiley College] then I began to learn that things were changing and things would change."[10]

By the time Johnson was in the White House, Wright was well enough known to rate reference in many contemporary writings of the Johnson administration. Her recipes appeared often in the food sections of newspapers, and her written challenge—served on a dinner plate in the White House—for the president to follow his diet and avoid another heart attack made newspapers all over the nation. Speaker of the House

Sam Rayburn called her "The best southern cook this side of Heaven."[11]

One can only assume that Wiley president Matthew Dogan saw something special in Zephyr Stephens that caused him to recommend her to Mrs. Johnson. Lady Bird's father, T.J. Taylor, was well known in the area, as was Lady Bird herself, so Dogan would have wanted the best of his Wiley students to accompany her to the nation's capital. Well educated and an excellent cook, she was well known to Johnson family intimates and probably had among the most recognized names of any member of a president's personal staff. Lyndon Johnson thus knew he could strike a chord of sympathy, especially among more moderate Southerners who admired her, when he used her as an icon of the need for the public accommodations portion of the Civil Rights Bill of 1964. He did it often.

Lady Bird Johnson

Claudia Alta Taylor was born in a small, northeastern Harrison County community called Karnack on December 22, 1912. A family servant said she was cute as a "Lady Bird," and the nickname stuck. Lady Bird may have come to her concern for civil rights through her mother, Minnie Lee Patillo Taylor, who was a suffragist as well as an integrationist.[12] After graduating from Marshall High School, Lady Bird Taylor eventually entered Texas University, graduating in 1934. She married Lyndon Johnson on November 17, 1934, and became, in his estimation as well as in others, one of his most effective campaigners. As Senate Majority Leader, he shepherded a Civil Rights Bill through the Congress. It may have been watered down—and Johnson certainly had a hand in weakening the enforcement provisions of it—but it was the first civil rights legislation passed since the constitutional amendments following the Civil War. Lady Bird herself recognized the significance of her husband's efforts and the rightness of his cause. In her *White House Diary*, she recalled those long days when she provided not only moral support, but actually brought him clean clothes and sustenance as he outlasted a southern-led filibuster to get the bill to Eisenhower's desk.[13]

The country got a close look at Lady Bird's character and vulnerability four days before the 1960 election when she and Lyndon went to Dallas to campaign. A right-wing Republican Congressman, Bruce Alger, had mobilized a group of women described by the press as "Junior League types, many in mink coats." They met the Johnsons in the lobby of the Baker Hotel and pursued them across the street to the Adolphus, where Johnson was to make a campaign speech, yelling at them and spitting on them both. "As Lady Bird was stepping out, one of the pickets impulsively snatched Mrs. Johnson's gloves from her hands and threw them in the gutter. Lady Bird went white. It was still a time when incivility was rare in politics, when public figures felt safe in crowds," wrote one eyewitness. With his wife tucked under his arm, as if to shield her from as much abuse as possible, Johnson slowly made his way across the lobby of the hotel, while television cameras recorded Lady Bird's discomfort, Johnson's embarrassed smile, and the jeering Republican women. Some say the scene convinced many northeastern voters that the Kennedy-Johnson ticket was worth their support.[14]

Neither Lady Bird nor Lyndon Johnson were racists, though Moyers said Johnson was known to tell racist jokes, "as was common at that time." Zephyr Wright, in her interview with Mike Gillette, agreed that the Johnsons, albeit Southern, were not racial bigots. Asked about the Johnson's attitude on race relations, she said, "They had to be easy to work with, because how do you think I worked for them for twenty-seven years if they hadn't been.... I think I noticed [their attitude] more during that time when Martin Luther King had that march on Washington. I didn't go, of course, because I think working for the Johnsons I didn't associate myself with any of these things that were going on. I kept it on TV, and President Johnson would come in and say, 'Did you hear what went on today?' and I said, 'Yes.' He just seemed happy with what was going on. He said, 'Well, this is a step forward for your people.'"[15]

Wright said she felt as though Johnson was unable to do what he wanted in regard to ending segregation because he could not ignore his constituents in Texas if he expected to be reelected. She could excuse Johnson but had problems with one of Johnson's mentors, Georgia Sen. Richard Russell. While intellectually she could accept the possibility that his public statements may have been motivated by the same forces that caused Johnson to weaken the 1957 Civil Rights Bill, still she seemed reluctant to tell Gillette her true feelings about the men who led the fight against the Civil rights Bill of 1964. "I must accept them the way they are because he accepts them. There is nothing else I can do about it."[16]

Passage of the Civil Rights Bill of 1964

Johnson began work on the Civil Rights Bill shortly after the assassination of Kennedy. The first word the nation had that Johnson would not return to his segregationist ways as Senate Majority Leader came in his address to a joint session of Congress on Wednesday, the day before Thanksgiving, 1963. In the gallery that evening was Zephyr Wright. She was among those who heard and applauded as her president denounced the "hate and evil and violence" of racism.[17]

Farmer received a presidential invitation to the White House. "I got a phone call from the president—at home—only three days after Kennedy's assassination," he said. "I had never been called by the president. I was highly flattered. This was my first experience with what people call the 'Johnson Treatment.' He let me know that he was going to need my help in the months and hopefully the years that lay ahead; and 'The next time you're in Washington, drop by and see me.'"[18]

Farmer's first face-to-face meeting with President Johnson was on December 3, 1963. He said he confronted the president with his less than sterling record on the passage of civil rights legislation and asked Johnson what had changed him. "Mr. Farmer, I'll answer that by quoting a friend of yours, 'Free at last. Free at last. Thank God A'mighty, I'm free at last.' What he was saying was that he was free from accountability to and reliance on any prejudiced constituency. Now he could act on his own feelings as president of the United States." Farmer said he was flattered by the Texas president's wooing of civil rights leaders. "Despite his southern accent and southern ways, he was sincerely for civil rights. And he was twisting arms, threatening, cajoling senators, lining up votes for the civil rights bill that became the Civil Rights Act of 1964." It was during this initial face-to-face meeting that Farmer first heard about the ordeal of Zephyr Wright. Johnson said that he felt the public accommodations portion was the heart and soul of the bill, and he told Farmer why.

> One day down in Texas many years ago my maid was going on vacation with her husband. Lady Bird—that's Mrs. Johnson, you know—told the maid to take our dog with her; we had a little beagle. My maid said, 'Mrs. Johnson, please don't make me take the dog with me. My husband and I will be driving across the South and it's going to be tough enough finding places to stay, just being black, without having a dog with us.'
>
> Mr. Farmer, that made me cry. Just to think that a wonderful woman like my maid couldn't stay in any hotel she wanted to. It made me mad. I'd lived in Texas all my life and I'd never thought about it before. Right then I swore that if I ever got any power, I would do something about it. Now I have the power and I'm going to do something about it.[19]

Johnson was trying to shepherd two important pieces of legislation through Congress at the same time; the civil rights bill and the antipoverty bill. He told Moyers on many occasions that he knew he would have to pick up some southern votes for the antipoverty legislation because some of the northern members of Congress would support civil rights but not the antipoverty measures. But they were votes he would not get if he angered southerners too severely, so he found himself walking a tightrope, not wanting to publically embarrass old colleagues but also unwilling to compromise the major provisions of the civil rights bill. One of the methods he used was to try to forestall as much criticism as possible of either measure.

Knowing that too many of his former southern Democratic colleagues would not support the Civil Rights Bill, Johnson began to court key Republicans. He needed them not only for the final vote, but more importantly, to end the filibusters that had killed every attempt at meaningful civil rights legislation in the past. "One man held the key to obtaining cloture: the minority leader of the Senate, Everett Dirksen," Johnson wrote in *The Vantage Point*. "Without his cooperation we could not enlist the support of moderate Republicans. And without Republican support we could not obtain the two-thirds vote necessary for cloture."[20] Lining up the support of Dirksen and other Republicans was a task to which Johnson enlisted the civil rights leaders. Farmer recalls meeting with Johnson on the matter:

> Mr. Farmer, I've got to get this civil rights bill through Congress, and I'm going to do it. If I never do anything else in my whole life, I'm going to get this job done. It won't be easy, but I'm going to do it. I have to get some of the Republicans on my side. You civil rights leaders can help me on that. You all should tell the Republicans that if they vote for this bill, you'll tell your people to vote for them. And I think you should, too, if they vote for this bill. You should tell people to vote for them.[21]

It was during this meeting, Farmer said, that he got another dose of "The Johnson Treatment." As Farmer listened, Johnson took a number of telephone calls from senators and representatives. "He twisted arms, threatened and cajoled, and then looked up to make sure I was duly impressed with his efforts on behalf of the bill."[22] At that point in their relationship, Farmer has said many times, he realized, if he had not before, that this southern president was truly committed to justice for all, despite the lack of support from the solid South, including most of

Johnson's Texas. The president made it clear that he was counting on Farmer's assistance.[23]

As the 1964 Civil Rights Bill moved inexorably through the house and senate, Farmer had particular reason to be concerned about Mississippi's well-documented racism. On Sunday, June 21, he received word that three CORE personnel had disappeared in Philadelphia in Neshoba County during "Freedom Summer," a CORE-SNCC (Student Nonviolent Coordinating Committee) project to register voters in the South. Michael Schwerner, age twenty-four, was a member of the CORE staff and Andrew Goodman, age twenty, was a CORE volunteer, as was native Mississippian James Chaney, twenty-two. Goodman and Schwerner, both from New York, were white and Chaney was black. While the FBI—and CORE—searched for the three civil rights workers, Farmer continued to support Johnson's efforts to pass the Civil Rights Bill. "It is possible for the president, from his position of moral authority as the leader of the American people to affect some changes—to set the tone of thought and feeling in the country.... What the president says is of upmost importance to the people," Farmer said in an interview at the LBJ Presidential Library in 1985. "So we told our [CORE] members and our supporters to fight, of course, for a president whose experiences, and whose background, and whose utterances, and whose records were more in common with what we wanted."[24]

On July 2, President Johnson signed into law the Civil Rights Bill of 1964. The violent deaths of those three CORE workers were among the major motivations for the second of Johnson's civil rights bills, the Voting Rights Bill of 1965. The signing ceremony took place in the East Room. A large delegation of civil rights leaders, senior members of the Justice Department, and members of Congress, including Texas Sen. Ralph Yarborough—the only southern senator to vote for the bill—gathered around the president. Of the four Marshallites, only Mrs. Johnson was present. Farmer, jailed in Louisiana, was the only major civil rights leader not in attendance at the signing; however, he and Moyers each played a role in the final chapter. Moyers wrote Johnson's widely reprinted speech delivered after the president used seventy-two ceremonial pens to sign the bill into law. Among the thousand words that emerged from Moyers' pen were these:

> The purpose of this law is simple. It does not restrict the freedom of any American so long as he respects the rights of others. It does not give special treatment to any citizen. It does say that the only limit to a man's hope for happiness and for the

future of his children shall be his own ability.

It does say that those who are equal before God shall now be also equal in the polling booths, in the classrooms, in the factories and in the hotels and restaurants and movie theaters and in other places that provide services to the public. . . . My fellow citizens, we have come to a time of testing. We must not fail. Let us close the springs of racial poison. Let us pray for wise and understanding hearts. Let us lay aside irrelevant differences and make our nation whole. . . . Let us hasten that day when our unmeasured strength and our unbounded spirit will be free to do the great works ordained to this nation by the just and wise God who is the Father of us all.[25]

On July 2, Farmer was in Kansas City, where CORE opened its national convention. He vowed to be the first to test the law with what he called "a civil rights haircut." Shortly after Johnson signed the bill into law, some of the delegates went down to the barbershop at the Muehlebach Hotel, site of the convention. That night, Farmer said, they were denied service, but the CORE director met with the hotel management, and the next morning, he said, the barber's union had provided barbers willing to comply with the newly enacted law. "I ordered the works—a shave and a haircut," Farmer said with a laugh thirty-four years later. "The barber soaped up my face, and when he got out his straight razor and put it up to my neck, I almost had second thoughts. But as I remember that was the best shave and haircut I ever got." [26]

The first lady made a whistle-stop tour of the South in October, during the campaign of 1964. At each stop, Mrs. Johnson's speech usually included, "We are a nation of laws, not men, and our greatness is our ability to adjust to the national consensus. The law to assure equal rights passed by Congress last July with three-fourths of the Republicans joining two-thirds of the Democrats, has been received by the South for the most part in a way that is a great credit to local leadership. . . . This convinces me of something I have always believed—that there is, in this Southland, more love than hate." Johnson won the 1964 election by one of the largest Electoral College votes on record. Perhaps through the First Lady's efforts, the South was at the least neutralized.[27]

Though he met with Johnson in the White House again, once with John Lewis regarding the Voting Rights Bill of 1965, Farmer was never able to mend fences destroyed when Farmer supported the Mississippi Freedom Democratic Party's effort to be seated at the 1964 convention. By the time Johnson signed the Voting Rights Bill of 1965—a bill largely inspired by the violence of Freedom Summer that had cost the lives of Farmer's volunteers, Goodman, Schwerner and Chaney—Farmer was such a persona-non-grata in the White House that Johnson almost refused to give the CORE director a ceremonial pen. "Martin and the others kept saying, 'What about Farmer? Give one to Farmer,'" Farmer said. "Finally he did, but he really didn't have a choice."[28]

Moyers said he was so caught up in the pace of the times that he had no idea the effect it would have on his hometown, and particularly on his parents. "People said some pretty harsh things to them at the time," Moyers said. "And my parents' neighborhood was one of the first to be integrated. But they never said a word to me in opposition, and they welcomed each new neighbor." It was not until the filming of *Marshall Texas/ Marshall Texas* that Moyers said he reflected on the impact the 1964 Civil Rights Act for the first time: "There really were two worlds. You could grow up well churched, well loved, well taught. We lived in the same small town, witnessed to the same faith—sang and prayed to the same God—and kept our distance. . . . You knew something was wrong, but you didn't want to admit it, even to yourself, or share it with others."[29]

NOTES

1. When asked by Moyers about the impact of the 1964 act, his high school English teacher, Inez Hughes, quoted a local banker. Hughes retired in 1964 rather than teach in an integrated school. "Marshall Texas/Marshall Texas, prod. David Grubin (episode of "Walk Through the 20th Century," ex. prods. Mort Kaplin and Charles Grinker). Corporation for Education and Learning (PBS, Jan. 1984).

2. Farmer Jr. and Wright were not the only students Tolson taught who challenged Jim Crow laws. Another was Houstonian Heman Marion Sweatt, the man who finally succeeded in integrating the law school at the University of Texas. According to Michael Gillette, "Sweatt's most inspiring teacher, however, was Melvin B. Tolson, the brilliant English professor. . . . Sweatt believed that no one, with the exception of his father, had influenced him as much as Tolson had. Sweatt was the plaintiff in a suit the NAACP filed in 1947 that was not settled until 1950, when the U.S. Supreme Court ruled the law school must integrated. A full account of Sweatt's case can be found in Michael Gillette, "Heman Marion Sweatt: Civil Rights Plaintiff," in *Black Leaders: Texans for Their Times*, ed. Alwyn Barr and Robert Calvert (Austin: Texas State Historical Association, 1981), 157-188.

3. With the *Irene Morgan v. Virginia* decision (1946) and the *Boynton v. Virginia* decision (1960) the U.S. Supreme Court declared segregation unconstitutional on interstate travel (*Morgan*) or in the facilities used to serve interstate travelers (*Boynton*). The Fellowship for Reconciliation (FOR) had staged a "Journey to Reconciliation" in 1947 to test the Morgan decision as to the integration of passengers on carriers, but the trip was only through the upper South. Farmer and CORE proposed to go deeper into the South to test both *Morgan* and *Boynton*. The steps leading to the final organization of the Freedom Rides as well as the Journey of Reconciliation can be found in James Farmer, *Lay Bare the Heart: An Autobiography of the Civil Rights Movement* (New York: Arbor House, 1985; reprint: Fort Worth: Texas Christian University Press, 1998), 195-196.

4. Farmer's account of the Freedom Rides can be found in *Lay Bare the Heart*. Farmer himself left the Freedom Ride because his father, stricken with cancer of the mouth and throat, died the night before the buses were to enter Alabama. John Lewis had also been on the first ride but left before the buses entered the Deep South. Both men rejoined the Freedom Rides and were jailed in Hinds County and then in Parchman Prison.

5. Soon after Moyers was hired, Cope got a complaint from one of the newspaper's advertisers, insurance man Piggy Byrne, that Moyers was too young to cover something as important as a school board meeting. The publisher suggested to his complainant that he wait until Moyers had actually covered the meeting and written his story to make a final judgment and to call back if the complainant still felt Moyers was too young. Byrne was never heard from again on the matter. Max Lale to Gail K. Beil, 1982, interview. Lale was city director of the *Marshall News Messenger* at the time Moyers was hired.

6. Eric Goldman, *The Tragedy of Lyndon Johnson* (New York: Alfred A. Knopf, 1969), 108.

7. Ibid.

8. Bill Moyers to Gail K. Beil, October 16, 1983, interview, notes in author's possession.

9. Patrick Anderson, The President's Men (Garden City, NJ: Doubleday and Co., 1969), 321.

10. Zephyr Wright to Mike Gillette, December 1974, interview 3-4. Wright name file text of AC 81 (tape 1 of 2) (Lyndon B. Johnson Presidential Library, Austin, Texas.)

11. Goldman, *Tragedy of Lyndon Johnson*, p. 351.

12. "What seemed downright incredible to Karnack, [Minnie Patillo Taylor] declared herself a suffragette and an integrationist of whites and blacks. Votes for women she could only talk about, but integration she practiced by inviting Negroes into the Brick House for long conversations, leaving T.J. Taylor shaking his head," in Goldman, *Tragedy of Lyndon Johnson*, 340.

13. "Lady Bird Johnson's Montage of Memories," *Marshall News Messenger*, May 13, 1978, Lady Bird Johnson file (Harrison County Historical Museum, Marshall, Texas); "LBJ," prod. David Grubin (episode of "The American Experience"), David Grubin Productions (PBS, 1992).

14. Lawrence Wright, "Growing up in Dallas," *Dallas Morning News*, Jan. 17, 1988, *Dallas Life Magazine*, 20.

15. Wright to Gillette, December 1974, interview, tape 1 transcript, 33-34. Wright name file text of AC 81 (tape 1 of 2) (LBJ Library). Moyers' opinion from Moyers to Beil, Aug. 10, 1997, interview, notes in author's possession.

16. Wright to Gillette, December 1974, interview, tape 1 transcript, 34.

17. Taylor Branch, *Pillar of Fire, America in the King Years 1963 to 1965* (New York: Simon and Schuster, 1998), 178.

18. "Marshall Texas/Marshall Texas."

19. Farmer, *Lay Bare the Heart*, 294.

20. Lyndon Baines Johnson, *The Vantage Point: Perspectives of the Presidency, 1963-1969* (New York: Holt, Rinehart and Winston, 1971), 158.

21. Farmer, *Lay Bare the Heart*, 293.

22. Ibid., 294.

23. LBJ's telephone logs as well as records of visitors to the White House confirm Farmer's recollections. Those records show that Johnson's most frequent visitor among the Big Four was Whitney Young. Telephone logs, November 1963 to July 2, 1964 (LBJ Library).

24. "Lyndon Johnson's Great Society—Part II—Civil Rights," audiotape R-1126 (LBJ Library).

25. *New York Times* and *Dallas Morning News*, July 3, 1964, front page, both papers.

26. Farmer to Beil, Jan. 13, 1998, interview. The account also appears on the front page of the *New York Times*, July 3, 1964, under the headline, "First Test of Law."

27. Liz Carpenter, *Ruffles and Flourishes: The Warm and Tender Story of a Simple Girl Who Found Adventure in the White House* (New York: Doubleday, 1970), 142.

28. Farmer to Beil, Aug. 9, 1997, interview, notes in author's possession.

29. "Marshall Texas/Marshall Texas."

East Texas and African American History: The Past and the Future

Cary Wintz

When it came my turn to prepare my presidential address, I was somewhat daunted by the prospect. I had twice previously served as a president of academic organizations, but the duties of office of neither required a presidential address. So, where to begin? My models were previous East Texas Historical Association (ETHA) presidential addresses, but they provided no real model. The principal characteristic was their difference. This ranged from humor and personal reflection to more traditional academic scholarship. All were effective and both entertaining and informative, but provided no real model I could adopt. What follows is my effort to present an informative and relevant discussion on an issue that is central to both East Texas History and the East Texas Historical Association—African American history. The original was based on a PowerPoint visual, consisting primarily of images and data. Later, an expanded version of this address was published as the foreword for Bruce Glasrud and Archie McDonald's collection, *Blacks in East Texas History*.

The study of African American history in East Texas, as well as the state of Texas has a checkered past. Prior to the second half of the twentieth century, African Americans and their history were rarely mentioned in either Texas history or U.S. history, especially in the major state, regional, and national historical associations, their conferences, and their journals. Slavery was discussed, as was Reconstruction. Otherwise, African Americans were almost invisible. Furthermore, the discussions of slavery and Reconstruction were very different from current interpretations. Slavery was generally depicted as a benign institution. Reconstruction histories contained little mention of African Americans players, and was generally presented as a needless and misguided effort of northerners to punish the defeated South, or inflict upon them corrupt and inefficient government. There was little, if any discussion of the segregation and disfranchisement of blacks following Reconstruction, and little or no material or discussion of African American leadership of the struggle against segregation and discrimination. Importantly, this narrative was not confined to Texas historians, but dominated the mainstream of American historical scholarship.

Two works illustrate the mainstream of historical thought in the state regarding African Americans in Texas history. The first was Charles William Ramsdell's *Reconstruction in Texas*, published with Columbia University Press in 1910. Ramsdell studied history at Columbia, wrote his dissertation under William Archibald Dunning, and was one of the charter members of the Dunning School of Reconstruction, which dominated Reconstruction history from the beginning of the twentieth century until World War II. Dunning sharply criticized Radical Reconstruction, military rule, and efforts to bestow political and civil rights on African Americans.

Ramsdell applied Dunning's teachings as the basis for his study of Reconstruction in Texas. He mentioned only one African American by name, George T. Ruby, who was one of the most influential black political leaders during Reconstruction. Ramsdell wrote that "there were only nine negro [sic] delegates, all save one from the black districts bordering the Brazos and Trinity Rivers. The exception was G.T. Ruby, of Galveston, a county predominately white. Ruby was a mulatto carpet-bagger from New England, a man of some ability and fair education, who generally led the negroes and threw his influence with the white carpet-baggers for the ultra-radical policies. He soon became the head of the Loyal Union League in Texas and was destined for fifteen years to be the political leader of his race in the state." Otherwise, except for mentioning the role of African American voters in the election of Republicans and radicals, and briefly discussing the Ku Klux Klan, which appeared in the state, especially in communities where the Loyal Union League "had produced restlessness" among blacks. He went on to minimize the violence of Klan activity, describing most as riding at midnight through black settlements in their ghostly costumes "disarming and frightening the superstitious freedmen out of their senses, but otherwise doing no harm." He acknowledged that sometimes Klan activities led to violence or even murder, but that in many cases violent persons "masquerading" as the Klan perpetrated the violence.

The second history that helped define the narrative of African American history in Texas was the first edition of Rupert Norval Richardson's text, *Texas: The Lone Star State*, published three decades after Ramsdell's work. Little had changed by 1943. Like his predecessors, Richardson included minimal material on African American history, and what he included focused on slavery and Reconstruction. Regarding the former, he wrote, "slaves fared better in Texas than in the older states.

. . . slaves were well treated. Women and children were given especial care." He also observed that because of the mobility of white citizens in Texas, slave "families were not often separated . . . Negroes had to endure the pangs of separation from loved ones far less frequently than did the white people. They were permitted to earn a reasonable amount of spending money, and they were rarely whipped."

Richardson's discussion of Reconstruction aligned with those of Dunning and Ramsdell. Regarding the abolition of slavery and the use of free black labor, he wrote, "of all their problems that of securing labor was greatest. Even if we make liberal allowances for the prejudices of the white men of that day against free Negro labor, we still cannot escape the conclusion that the freedmen were very inefficient. Almost without exception, reports for the first four years describe the Negro laborers as 'indolent,' 'listless,' and 'almost worthless.'" Richardson concluded that the efficiency of African American labor did not improve until the removal of the Freedmen's Bureau in 1868 and the replacement of the wage labor system with the practice of leasing or renting land to blacks, which was institutionalized by 1870 in the sharecropping system.

Richardson concluded his discussion of Reconstruction with the assertion that it had a negative impact on African Americans and worsened race relations. He argued that the social experiment of bestowing rights on blacks, especially the right to vote, was a misguided experiment of "standing the social pyramid on its apex," and that bestowing the right to vote occurred too suddenly. He also claimed Governor Davis' use of a desegregated state militia and police force exasperated racial conflict: "If he [E.J. Davis] had sought deliberately to provoke disturbances in order to provide an excuse for declaring martial law, he could not have found a better device than the use of a state constabulary made up in the main of officious white adventurers and Negroes." He also argued that the effects of the Texas Constitution of 1869 and the Fifteenth Amendment "were to disfranchise the Negro." He went on to assert that, "racial tensions were seriously aggravated by reconstruction; and the evil effects of it have not been overcome altogether even to this day. Before the Civil War, to mistreat a Negro stamped a white man as . . . 'po white trash'; during the reconstruction era, the Negro-hater often became a hero."

Richardson discussed African Americans in Texas in only two other contexts. First, he justified the disfranchisement of blacks through the 1905 Terrell Election Law because of the alleged corruption of the party primaries. "During Lanham's administration," he wrote, "the legislature took hold of the problem in earnest. Two laws, named after Judge A.W. Terrell, their author, improved the fairness and honesty of both primaries and general elections." Richardson also discussed the "white primary" law of 1923, and the unsuccessful Supreme Court challenges to this and subsequent laws. The second context involved the progress that African Americans had made since emancipation. Here, he focused on social progress, noting that in education, although black schools have operated under severe handicaps, "Negro leaders have toiled faithfully . . . . . And the Negro People have made substantial improvement." He also observed that African American material progress has not kept pace with educational progress, and he noted the demographic shift of African American from rural Texas to urban areas and the overall decline of African Americans as a percent of the state's population.

In 1958, fifteen years after the first edition, Richardson published his second edition of *Texas: The Lone Star State*. Much had happened since the first edition. Two civil rights cases outlawed the Texas white primary and desegregated professional education in Texas, the *Brown* case declared school segregation illegal, President Eisenhower used federal troops to desegregate public schools in Little Rock, and Congress was in the process of enacting the first federal civil rights law since the end of Reconstruction. However, to a large degree, the interpretation of slavery and Reconstruction remained unchanged. Richardson used the exact wording on the relatively benign nature of Texas slavery cited above from his first edition. His discussion of Reconstruction was almost identical to that of the first edition, although he moderated slightly his language regarding the use of the state militia, and the ineffectiveness of African American labor. His general condemnation of the long-term impact of Reconstruction on race relations remained unchanged.

Richardson again discussed the Terrell election laws and the imposition of the white primary, but concluded with *Smith v. Allwright*, and the final Supreme Court decision overturning the white primary. The discussion of black progress in the mid-twentieth century expanded to include African American higher education, the desegregation of the University of Texas Law School, and the early struggle to desegregate public education and higher education, as well as the white efforts against the progress. These changes reflected recognition of the beginnings of the modern civil rights movements, the successes of African Americans in some areas, and the resistance of a large number of white Texans to the changes. Richardson's tone, for the most part, is descriptive and neutral. He describes desegregation as relatively peaceful, with visible progress in higher education, schools, and in West Texas.

The most significant changes in writing the history of African Americans in Texas began with the production of a series of dissertations and books from Texas scholars beginning in the late 1960s. This phenomenon began in 1967 with Lawrence D. Rice's dissertation, "The Negro in Texas, 1874-1900," completed at Texas Tech University under the direction of Lawrence Graves. This dissertation was a study of the crucial post-Reconstruction era, and it was the first of a series of dissertations and books from Texas Tech graduate students and faculty that launched the professional study of African American history in Texas.

Rice published his dissertation under the same title with Louisiana State University Press in 1971. That same year, Alwyn Barr, a new faculty member at Texas Tech, published *Black Texans: A History of Negroes in Texas, 1528-1971*, the first and still, the only complete survey of African American history from the era of Spanish exploration to the present. Other graduate students and faculty working on African American history at Texas Tech at the time included Bruce Glasrud, "Black Texans, 1900-1930: A History" (1969), and James Smallwood, whose *Time of Hope, Time of Despair: Black Texans during Reconstruction* (1981) addressed all the issues of Reconstruction that Ramsdell overlooked, and in analysis deviated significantly from the Dunning school. That same year, Alwyn Barr and Robert Calvert produced their edited collection of biographical essays, *Black Leaders: Texans for their Times* (1981).

The impact of these Texas Tech historians on African American history proved to be pivotal, both because of their pioneering work and because they opened the door for a rapidly growing number of historians who followed in their footsteps and added significantly to the rapidly growing number of publications on the African American experience in Texas. The early studies that came out of Texas Tech tended to be chronological in nature, surveying African American history in specific time periods, while the work of the historians that followed tended to be more focused monographs on a wide variety of topics, including individuals, locations, and specific aspects of African American history. For example, Merline Pitre (along with Ruthe Winegarten and others) brought African American women into the center of African American history in Texas. Pitre's biographical study of Houston NAACP leader Lulu White raised questions about gender and leadership in the African American community. She also wrote a study of African American political leadership in post-Reconstruction Texas. Neil Foley showed the complexity of race and agricultural labor in his study of the racialization of poor whites, blacks, and Mexicans in the commercial agricultural industry of South Texas. Additionally, Tom Cole reconstructed the "secret" history of the sit-in movement that desegregated Houston's public accommodations, and demonstrated that the civil rights movement was an assortment of local movements operating with little or no national input.

Three African American scholars followed and produced pioneering books on African American social history and economic topics. Their academic roots were in Houston and Southeast Texas, rather than West Texas. Ernest Obadele-Starks examined the operations of the Fair Employment Practice Committee (FEPC) and its impact on the upper Texas Gulf Coast industries during the 1940s. Pres. Franklin Roosevelt created the federal committee to head off A. Phillip Randolph's threatened 1940 March on Washington. This Texas case study examined the impact of the FEPC on the area of the former Confederacy with the largest concentration of black industrial workers. The FEPC represented the first effort to impose desegregation as part of national policy and brought racial issues into the study of Texas labor history. Amilcar Shabazz focused his efforts on the struggle to desegregate higher education in Texas. His book provided insight into the status of higher education for Texas blacks in the early twentieth century as well as the effort to end segregation in higher education. Dwight Watson examined race and its impact on the Houston Police Department during the turbulent, lengthy civil rights struggle. It exposed both the complexity of race issues within the police department and the role of the police department in addressing race in the city of Houston. These three historians each had connections to Texas Southern University. Watson and Starks received their masters degrees in history there prior to receiving their doctorates in history at the University of Houston, while Shabazz worked as an adjunct instructor at Texas Southern while completing his degree, also at the University of Houston.

Bruce Glasrud, one of the original Texas Tech doctoral students who pioneered the study of African American history in Texas, continued throughout his career to contribute to the discipline. In addition to his many books and edited collections on the subject, he is the premier bibliographer of African American history in Texas and the West. His most comprehensive bibliographical work is the study he coauthored with Laurie Champion, *Exploring the Afro-Texas Experience*, which contained an exhaustive list and discussion of secondary sources on African American history in Texas.

Complementing and supporting the work of the individual historians who researched and published the work on African American Texas history were the publishers and professional organizations that supported this work. Of these, perhaps the most significant is the East Texas Historical Association through the *East Texas Historical Journal*.

Beginning in 1971 (when Archie McDonald assumed the editorship) through 2005, the *Journal* has published forty-two articles on African American history, including one issue entirely devoted to the topic. The *East Texas Historical Journal* publishes two issues per year. From 1971 through 2005, the seventy issues contained forty-two articles on the subject of black history. In other words, during this period approximately sixty percent of the issues of the *East Texas Historical Journal* contained an article on African American history. Not surprisingly, three of the early Texas Tech graduate students, Bruce Glasrud, Jim Smallwood, and Neil Sapper, published essays in the journal, and Texas Southern University faculty member, Merline Pitre, became the first African American scholar to do so in 1988. In addition to its journal, the ETHA also supported scholarship in African American history though papers presented at its spring and fall conferences.

The role of East Texas, the East Texas Historical Association, and its journal in promoting African American History in Texas is appropriate. As a region, East Texas has a disproportional number of African American population, university students, and faculty, as noted in Table 1 below.

Table 1
Higher Education Demographics, I

	Texas	East Texas
Percent Black Population	11.5%	16.4%
Black University Students	10.8%	17.6%
Black Faculty	4.8%	7.6%
Tenured Black Faculty	4.3%	6.6%

As this illustrates, East Texas, roughly defined as the region north of the Brazos River and East of the Interstate 35 corridor, has a denser population of African Americans than the state of Texas as a whole. In addition, the data regarding African American participation in higher education seems to indicate that they are more highly represented in East Texas. Most notable, the percent of African American participation in higher education in East Texas is greater than their percent of the East Texas population. Additionally, African American faculty members are fifty percent more likely to achieve tenure in East Texas. Unfortunately, the data in Table 1 is misleading.

Table 2
Higher Education Demographics, II

	East Texas	Excluding HBCUs
Percent Black Population	16.4%	
Black University Students	17.6%	11.2%
Black Faculty	7.6%	3.4%
Tenured Black Faculty	6.6%	2.4%

Table 2 provides a different picture of black educational participation in East Texas. East Texas is the home of Texas's two public historical black institutions of higher education: Texas Southern University in Houston, and Prairie View A&M University, thirty miles northwest of Houston. When data from these two institutions is withdrawn, the picture of black participation in higher education changes dramatically. The percent of African American students who attend non-HBCUs in East Texas is about the same as it is in the rest of the state. The percent of black faculty employed in non-HBCUs is significantly lower than it is in the rest of the state, as is the percent of black faculty who gain tenure. The following data, drawn from the same sources as Table 1 and Table 2, more clearly illustrate the distribution of African Americans in higher education in East Texas. Of the African American students enrolled in higher education in East Texas in the fall 2003, forty-two percent attended either Texas Southern or Prairie View A&M; fifty-eight percent attended the other colleges and universities in East Texas. For African American faculty, the data are even worse. Fifty-eight percent of African American faculties are employed at Texas Southern and Prairie View A&M, and sixty-six percent of the tenured African American faculties work at the two HBCUs. Consequently, only thirty-four percent of the tenured African American faculties in East Texas teach at non-HBCUs.

What does this mean? Despite the growth and quality of the scholarship on African American history in Texas and the significant role that the ETHA has played in supporting this scholarship, racial disparity still exists in Texas and East Texas. This is particularly a problem in the employment and tenure of faculty in East Texas colleges and universities.

When I presented this talk at the September 2005 meeting of the East Texas Historical Association, I concluded with a pointed question.

While acknowledging the significant role that the association played in fostering and supporting African American history, I asked my audience to look around them and see how many African American historians were in the room. I could see from the podium that among the 100 or so historians present, only two were African Americans. I concluded my talk with the comment that we still have a lot of work to do.

Happily, I can report that there has been significant progress since my presentation. A couple of years after my talk, an African American historian stood at the podium and delivered the presidential address at the fall meeting of the association. In addition, the participation of African American scholars and graduate students has continued to increase. The annual breakfast meeting of historians working on African American history has become a popular feature of the all meeting. The future looks bright.

R.L. MOORE: LEGENDARY MATHEMATICIAN AND TEACHER

R. G. Dean

Presidential address to the fall meeting of the East Texas Historical Association, Friday, September 22, 2006, at the Hotel Fredonia in Nacogdoches, Texas.

Good Evening. Thanks for being here. Before I say anything else, I want to express to you how much it means to have the opportunity to serve as your president. In my life, there have been a lot of things I wanted to happen to me, or which I expected to happen to me, which have not happened—and possibly never will. And there have been a lot of things which I never expected to happen to me which have, and some have been bad and some were good, but having the opportunity to serve as your president is something I never, in my wildest dreams, thought might happen—and it has been one of those good things!

As a few of you know, but most of you probably do not, I made my living, for over four decades, doing and teaching mathematics. I seriously doubt that any of my history teachers, in either high school or college, would have expected me to even attend a meeting of historians, and certainly not to be asked to serve as an officer, so thank you.

This brings me closer to the point of what I am to talk about tonight. One bit of advice that I have been given is to talk about something I know about. Well, I probably know more about mathematics and mathematicians than anything else. My area of specialization was abstract algebra, and my dissertation was a study of properties of an abstract algebraic system called semirings. Semirings were first studied and named by Harry S. Vandiver at the University of Texas in 1936. Harry Vandiver was the father of historian Frank Vandiver, who I suspect many of you know or at least recognize.

Unless there are more "closet mathematicians" here than I am aware of, if I were to talk about semirings, possibly the only people in the hall who would be able to enjoy my talk are Greg Beil, Karon O'Neil, and our son, Keith Dean. So, I am not going to talk about semirings.

Let me tell you a little ancient history instead. When I was a first year teacher in high school, I had a colleague who used to tell me stories about a famous professor at the University of Texas who had a really unusual way of teaching. He told me stories about how you could pass classrooms on the third floor of Benedict Hall and find groups of students standing out in the hall while class was going on. Now, bear in mind, these were college classes and some of them were even graduate classes. He told me that the teacher in that classroom was named R.L. Moore. Now, what kind of teacher was this R.L. Moore who would banish his students from the classroom while class was going on? What kind of teacher was he, indeed?

Over the years, as I came into contact with more former students from UT, I heard more and more R.L. Moore stories. Like the one about the time The American Mathematical Society published a book by Moore about his work. The story says that when the UT Library received its copy of the book, the librarian called Dr. Moore to tell him that they had a copy of his book, whereupon Moore went over and checked it out—and never returned it! And there were stories about how Moore would kick a student out of his class if he found out they were using the library or any other research sources when doing their homework. What kind of teacher was he, indeed?

Who was R.L. Moore? When Robert Lee Moore was born on November 14, 1882, Texas had been in the Union for fewer than 37 years. The War Between the States had been over for a mere seventeen years. Born in Dallas, Moore was the fifth of six children for Charles Jonathan and Louisa Ann Moore. Sam Bass, the infamous Robin Hood train robber had been killed in Round Rock, Texas only five years earlier. Carrie Nation was still operating a hotel in Richmond, Texas. The University of Texas had not yet taught its first class. Dallas was still a frontier town with open saloons in which buttermilk had become a very popular drink. The Dallas Telephone Exchange was established in June 1881 and about 260 hand-operated phones were immediately put to use. In 1882, the year of R.L. Moore's birth, the first electric light plant in Dallas was put into operation and electric street cars came to Dallas, but horses were still the principal mode of transportation. In 1882, the first paving of streets was done when Elm Street and Main Street were paved with bois d'arc blocks. In 1882, Sanger Brothers was offering men's worsted suits for $10.50 each, and the first public schools were still five years in the future.

Charles J. Moore was a strong-willed man who had been born in New England, near Hartford, Connecticut. Before the beginning of the Civil War, he and a brother moved to Kentucky, and when the war started, he joined the Southern cause, volunteering for service in the armies of the Confederacy, serving in the Orphan Brigade, Company A, Second Kentucky Regiment. Charles Moore was so devoted to the Southern cause that he concealed the fact he had been born in New England until it was discovered by accident when his children were grown. After the war, Charles J. Moore met and married Louisa Ann Moore and migrated toward the West, finally settling in Dallas. He operated a hardware store and feed company in a central location in downtown Dallas. It was just off the town square and faced the site of the courthouse. In fact, by 1882, a fourth courthouse was being constructed almost directly across the street from the Moore feed and hardware store. Years later, shots would ring out over the site of the old Moore store as John F. Kennedy, president of the United States, was assassinated.

Schooling in the late 1800s in Dallas was not well organized. Many parents, who could afford to, sent their children to private schools, often run by a headmaster or principal. Often one person, or maybe a husband and wife would teach all the subjects. Robert Lee Moore studied with a man named Waldemar Malcolmson. Reportedly, on one occasion a parent, W.H. Flippin, brought his two sons to enroll in Malcolmson's school. As the parent was leaving, Malcolmson called after him and said, "Oh, Mr. Flippen , how do you want the earth taught, flat or round? I can teach it both ways."

Moore began school with Malcolmson when he was eight and studied with him until he was barely fifteen. His studies included such subjects as Spanish and shorthand, as well as other fundamental subjects. After learning shorthand, he habitually wrote notes to himself in the margins of his books. Before Moore was fifteen years old, he had decided to enroll at the University of Texas. Malcolmson did not teach Latin, nor did he offer calculus. Since Moore needed Latin for entrance into the newly established University of Texas, he dropped out of Malcolmson's school in order to study independently those subjects he needed to enter the University. Since he planned to study mathematics, he borrowed a calculus book from his teacher, with which he began his study of calculus, but he soon lost patience with the imprecise language of the text, so he wrote to the University of Texas requesting a copy of the calculus book used there. His method of studying calculus, using the book sent to him, was natural for him. He would read a statement of a theorem, but would use a card to cover the portion of the page that gave the proof of the theorem. Then he would attack the theorem on his own. If, after what he felt a reasonably long time went by without success in proving the theorem, he would then uncover the first line of the proof, read that, and then try to prove the theorem without further assistance. If this failed, he would uncover the next line and continue in that fashion until he had obtained a proof. He enrolled in the University in 1898, a few weeks before his sixteenth birthday.

Throughout his life, R.L. Moore had an aversion to reading the work of other mathematicians. This aversion was to contribute strongly to his research methods and similarly to his teaching method. Even though he would sometimes attend lectures, it was his practice to ignore the speaker and either work on problems of his own or else work on his own proof of whatever the lecturer was proving.

"The total enrollment of academic students at UT by 1897 was 408. The library held approximately 2640 volumes and the university authorities claimed [an] earnest desire to reduce to the lowest possible point the expense of education. Many of the students supported themselves by doing work in private families, milking cows, making fires, cooking, tending the horses; others waited on the tables in boarding houses or attended to the rooms; others taught, acted as clerks, stenographers, typists, accountants, or surveyors." One of the most significant influences on Moore at the niversity was the eminently qualified but notably eccentric professor of pure and applied mathematics, George Bruce Halsted, who had earned his MA from Princeton and his Ph.D. from Johns Hopkins University. When Moore arrived at the university, he was already strong willed and largely self-educated. Quick of mind, already with a driving interest in and dedication to mathematics, he was placed by Halsted in calculus. After a short period of time when it became evident that calculus was not sufficiently challenging, Halsted transferred Moore to his course in projective geometry. Thus, in his freshman year he was already in competition with juniors and seniors.

Reportedly, Halsted seldom lectured, and when he did, it was rarely about mathematics. He would speak of his travels, his experiences, and his attitudes with little reservation, a trait that would later cost him his job at the University of Texas. His class management was to call on students to explain passages in the textbook. Usually, some assignments came from the text, and Halsted would commence by asking a student to explain some statement from that section. If, for example, a phrase began in the text with the statement, "It is obvious that," he would call on a student and ask why it was obvious. A popular joke among mathematicians has a professor making the statement that such-and-such is obvious. When a student asks, "Is that really obvious?," the professor would say, "Well, yes, I think so," and then lapse into deep concentration for several minutes before suddenly leaving the room without a word. After about a half hour, he returned, and upon entering the room, announced, "Yes, it is obvious," and then resumed his lecture. In the case of Halsted, if no answer was forthcoming, he would call on another member of the class, asking, "Mr._____, will you explain why that is obvious?" After inquiring of several other students, without success, he would then be likely to say, "All right, Mr. Moore, Why is it obvious?"

A teacher who did not lecture, but rather expected students to study independently was evidently just what Moore needed. About Halsted, Moore would later say, "There is no other person I would have wished to study under; that is, if someone should ask me if I wouldn't rather have studied under Professor X, and they named <u>any other person</u>, then I would say, 'No!'" Needless to say, Robert Lee Moore did well at the University of Texas, and he completed his Bachelor of Science degree in 1901 at the ripe young age of eighteen. He remained there through the academic year 1901-02 as a Fellow in pure mathematics. Halsted recommended Moore for a position in the Mathematics Department for the academic year 1902-03, but the board of regents refused to hire him. The denial was probably more because Halsted had angered the administration than because of anything Moore had done. The disappointed Moore thus accepted a teaching position at a high school in Marshall in East Texas.

Meanwhile, the eminent mathematician, Eliakim Hastings Moore (no relation to R.L. Moore) became the head of the Department of Mathematics at the University of Chicago, where he developed a reputation for bringing to his department the most fertile of minds, both on the faculty and in the student body. By April 1902, R.L. Moore had made a significant contribution as a mathematics researcher. Halsted had suggested a problem to one of his classes, which led R.L. Moore to prove that one of David Hilbert's geometry axioms was redundant. Many of you will remember from your high school geometry classes that Euclid devised a list of basic assumption on which his geometry, what we now call Euclidean Geometry, was based. The axioms for Euclidean Geometry are:

- Any two *points* can be joined by a *straight line*.

- Any *straight line segment* can be extended indefinitely in a straight line.

- Given any straight line segment, a *circle* can be drawn having the segment as *radius* and one endpoint as center.

- All *right angles* are *congruent*.

- *Parallel postulate*. If two lines intersect a third in such a way that the sum of the *inner angles* on one side is less than two right angles, then the two lines inevitably must intersect each other on that side if extended far enough.

Ideally, a set of axioms should be self-evident (i.e. requiring no proof), and independent, meaning no one of them can be proved by using the others. During the late nineteenth century, mathematicians were investigating some non-Euclidean geometries—geometrical systems which did not satisfy the set of axioms used by Euclid. Two notable examples were geometries, which used axioms one to four but made assumptions different from axiom five.

David Hilbert, one of the greatest mathematicians up until his time, had a set of axioms that he believed to be independent, but R.L. Moore proved in 1902 that one of Hilbert's axioms could be proved using his other axioms. This brought R.L. Moore to the attention of E.H. Moore, whose research interests at the time were on the foundations of geometry, so he arranged a scholarship that would allow Robert Moore to study for his doctorate in Chicago. Since R.L. Moore had already accepted a position in Marshall, he delayed his entry into the University of Chicago for a year; however, R.L. Moore received his Ph. D. at the University of Chicago in 1905 for a dissertation titled *Sets of Metrical Hypotheses for Geometry* under the supervision of Oswald Veblen. Moore was then just twenty-two.

According to F. Burton Jones, one of Moore's students, it was while Moore was at Chicago that he first hit on his unique teaching methods. Jones said, "With his quick mind and restless spirit he found the lecture method rather boring—in fact, mind dulling. To liven up a lecture he would run a race with his professor by seeing if he could discover the proof of an announced theorem before the lecturer had finished his presentation. Quite frequently, he won the race, but in any case, he felt that he was better off from having made the attempt. [F. Burton Jones, "The Moore Method," *The American Mathematical Monthly* 84 (4) (1977), 273-277.]

After graduating from Chicago, Moore spent a year as an assistant professor at the University of Tennessee, two years as an instructor at Princeton University, and three years as an instructor at Northwestern University. In 1910, Moore married Margaret MacLelland Key of Brenham, Texas, and in 1911, he went to the University of Pennsylvania as an instructor and received an appointment to assistant professor in 1916. According to Burton Jones, it was at the University of Pennsylvania that Moore first tried out his teaching methods in a Foundations of Geometry course he taught. He began to have success with what became the Moore Method of teaching, also sometimes called the Discovery Method.

In 1915, Moore published in the *Transactions of the American Mathematical Society* a set of axioms sufficient to define a number plane. Its publication in *Transactions* was an indication of the significance of the work, and by 1920, he had published seventeen papers on point-set topology, a term he coined. Simply stated, topology is the study of the properties of a mathematical system that remain unchanged by continuous deformations.

In 1920, Moore joined the faculty of the University of Texas, where he had been denied a position as a lecturer eighteen years earlier. He began as an associate professor and in 1923 received promotion to full professor. In 1932, the American Mathematical Society published his book, *Foundations of Point Set Topology*. It was this book that he reportedly checked out of the university library and never returned. The two leading organizations of mathematicians are the American Mathematical Society (AMS) and the Mathematical Association of America (MAA). The former has traditionally focused on the works of research mathematicians, with the latter directed toward teachers of mathematics. In 1929, Moore was a colloquium speaker at the AMS, and he was elected to the National Academy of Sciences in 1931. In 1937 and 1938, he served as president of the American Mathematical Society. Moore was an editor of the Colloquium Publications from 1929 to 1936, being editor-in-chief from 1930 to 1933. In the principal publication of the MAA, Burton Jones attempted to describe the Moore Method of teaching.

> Moore would begin his graduate course in topology by carefully selecting the members of the class. If a student had already studied topology elsewhere or had read too much, he would exclude him. . . he wanted the competition to be as fair as possible, for competition was one of the driving forces. . . .
>
> Having selected the class he would tell them briefly his view of the axiomatic method . . . . He would then state the axioms that the class was to start with . . . .
>
> After stating the axioms and giving motivating examples to illustrate their meaning he would then state some definitions and theorems. . . . He would then instruct the class to find proofs of their own and also to construct examples to show that the hypotheses of the theorems could not be weakened, omitted, or partially omitted.
>
> . . . for the next meeting he would call on some student to prove Theorem 1. After he became familiar with the abilities of the class members, he would call on them in reverse order [of their abilities] and in this way give the more unsuccessful students first chance when they did get a proof.
>
> [If] a student stated that he could prove Theorem x, he

was asked to go to the blackboard and present his proof. Then the other students, especially those who had not been able to discover a proof, would make sure that the proof presented was correct and convincing. Moore sternly prevented heckling. [If a student was still working on a proof and did not want to see someone else's proof, that student was allowed to retire to the hallway during the presentation, thus the groups of students standing in the hallway outside Moore's classroom.]

When a flaw appeared in a "proof," everyone would patiently wait for the student at the board to "patch it up." If he could not, he would sit down. Moore would then ask the next student to try or . . . he would save that theorem until next time and go on to the next unproved theorem (starting again at the bottom of the class).

This teaching method epitomized Moore's approach to both teaching and research. A popular quote attributed to him is, "That student is taught the best who is told the least." And a Chinese proverb which was a favorite of Moore's, went, "I hear, I forget. I see, I remember. I do, I understand."

Not everything about Moore is admirable. There were those who accused him of being both a sexist and a racist. Doubtless, there was some truth to the accusation during part of his career. After all, he grew up in the house of a Confederate veteran who tried to hide the fact that he was born in New England. Regardless, Moore had Ph. D. students who were women and at least one student who was Jewish. He had no graduate students who were black, however. Mary Ellen Rudin, one of his female students said of Moore's teaching method, "His way of teaching was to present you with things that had not yet been proved, and with all kinds of things which might turn out to have a counterexample, and sometimes unsolved problems—that is, unsolved by anyone, not only unsolved by you. So you had some idea of what it meant to be a mathematician—more than the average undergraduate does today." Although the Moore Method worked for her, she also said, "I wouldn't for anything have let my children go to school with Moore! That is, I think that he was destructive to anyone who didn't fit exactly into his pattern, he did not succeed in giving the people that worked with him an education. It's a mistake to go to school under those circumstances in general."

Vivienne Mayes-Malone, a Ph.D. from the University of Texas at Austin, said she could not enroll in Professor R.L. Moore's class, as he explicitly stated that he did not teach blacks. Walker E. Hunt, also a Ph.D. from the University of Texas at Austin, said "I also wanted to take Robert E. Lee Moore's famous, Foundations of Point-Set Topology. However, that was not to be. The reason, I was black! His words were, 'You are welcome to take my course but you start with a C and can only go down from there.'"

How did he get away with such behavior? There is no doubt he was a formidable force at the University of Texas. His graduate students had private offices, while most faculty members doubled up. Most faculty members taught two, three, or four sections per semester, while Moore taught five or six. There was a rule at the university that after retiring at age seventy, a professor could continue to teach halftime year to year upon the recommendation of the departmental budget council. In 1952, Moore was seventy years old, but he taught until 1969 when he was eighty-six years old. He wanted to continue teaching even then, but university authorities forced him to retire. It was Dean J.R. Silber who finally took it upon himself to get rid of Moore. Some believe he was motivated by personal animosity and others believe he was only removing a roadblock to continued growth of the Mathematics Department.

It is not too surprising a fact that it had become difficult to recruit capable young mathematicians to a faculty dominated by Moore. As an example, one of Moore's most successful students, R.H. Bing, was a topologist of world-renowned stature, and Texas desperately wanted to attract him back from Wisconsin. Word was that Bing said he would never return to Texas while Moore was there, and a year or so after Moore died, Bing did in fact return to Texas.

Many of Moore's students and former students vigorously fought the dismissal of Moore. In his defense, they compiled a 155-page monograph detailing correspondence and conversations concerning Moore, refuting the charges Dean Silber made against him. Silber reportedly said Moore had been unable to place any of his students in a leading university in twenty-five years, that he had not had a major publication in more than a quarter of a century, and that none of his students in the past decade had any significant publications. Some relevant facts though are that few mathematicians publish more than two papers. Moore published more than sixty papers and a couple of books. Few mathematicians ever publish after the age of sixty, but Moore published four papers after reaching that age. At the age of eighty, he published a book on topology described as superlative in its field. Moore graduated fifty Ph.D students, thirty-four of them after he was sixty; twenty-five after he was seventy, and fourteen after he was eighty. Not only was Moore named to the National Academy of Sciences, but so too were three of his students: Raymond L. Wilder, Gordon T. Whyburn, and R.H. Bing. No other professor, and not even another university, has had such distinction. In 1967, the Mathematical Association of America released a film, *"Challenge in the Classroom,"* extolling the teaching and the teaching method of R.L. Moore. As for his recent students who were supposedly unable to produce significant publications, the seven who graduated from 1957 to 1963 had a combined total of forty-nine publications in reputable mathematics journals. The mathematical genealogy of R.L. Moore reads like that of one of the biblical patriarchs. He had fifty doctoral students and now has a total (as of today) of 2,049 Ph.D. descendants.

As you might imagine, there is a wealth of folklore about R.L. Moore. I will include one story that I have not tried to verify. It sounds so much like R.L. Moore that I just want to believe it is true. Moore was unusually healthy and seldom missed a class. Once when he was well into his eighties, he failed to show up for a one o'clock seminar. His students were so dedicated to him that they were not about to "walk" when he was late. A half hour passed and Moore failed to show. An hour passed and some of the students began to get nervous; some of them had five or six years invested in studying under Moore. What if he had had a heart attack and died? What would become of them if their major professor was gone? Eventually, some of them got concerned enough to telephone his home to inquire about him. Moore was not dead and he had not had a heart attack. What had happened was that the Moores had a large tree in their back yard that needing cutting down. When he found out it would cost two hundred dollars to get it cut, he decided to do the job himself. He tackled the job with the saw he had, and it was not a power saw. He eventually got the tree down, but it was well past midnight, and he was so exhausted, he had slept through the class the next afternoon. The reason it had taken so long was that at some earlier time, the tree was hollow, and the hollow space filled with cement. This incident proved once again that Robert Lee Moore was independent and not a quitter.

The university forcibly retired Moore in 1969. On the last day of the summer session that year, Robert Lee Moore taught his last class at Texas. The class closed and no student moved, as if they could prevent it from happening by not leaving. Finally, Moore walked from the room. In 1972, the university honored Moore, against his wishes, with the dedication of the Robert Lee Moore Hall, home of the physics, mathematics, and astronomy departments at the corner of Dean Keeton and Speedway on the UT campus. He did not want the building named for him—he wanted to teach in it, or better yet, in Benedict Hall. R.L. Moore suffered a stroke in May 1974 followed by a second stroke in June. He died in Austin on October 4, 1974, just a few weeks before his ninety-second birthday.

Steve Allen Never Picked Cotton in Texas

Dan K. Utley

Festus and Mabel. Sounds like a lost episode of *Gunsmoke* or maybe a California folk music duo from the 1960s. Festus and Mabel. Perhaps a Martin Scorsese film of life along the Brooklyn waterfront or a Willa Cather novel about a young girl coming of age in Festus, Missouri. Festus and Mabel, though—more precisely Festus John, Jr. and Blanche Mabel Prater Utley—were my parents. Both grew up on cotton farms in Bell County, Texas, and they lived their early lives only about a dozen miles apart along the blackland prairie in the central part of the state. Festus John Utley, Sr., who came to Texas as a young man from North Carolina, seeking unspoiled farmland and economic opportunity, died a young man, the result of complications from a farming accident on his land. My father, only a year old when his father died, grew up picking cotton, but his mother eventually turned the homeplace over to sharecroppers and moved into the big city of Belton. As a result, my father was soon able to put his cotton-picking past behind him.

My mother, however, was another story, and it is her influence that sets the personal context for this paper. To her, cotton picking was something akin to a Marine Corps boot camp. It was the touchstone of her youth, and it influenced her work ethic throughout her life in interesting ways. It was an integral means by which she measured one's character or values, as well as a job's degree of difficulty. To her, those who picked cotton were automatically part of an undefined but universal fraternal organization, and they had successfully passed the initiation—no password necessary.

Festus and Mabel married in 1937 and eventually made their way the following decade to the East Texas town of Lufkin, where I was born. Although I did not have the opportunity to pick cotton, I grew up taking on other jobs. I ran a printing press, sacked groceries, worked on a hay baling crew, hauled honey bees, fixed flats in a gas station, poisoned trees in the Tyler County swamps around Hillister, and even worked one day in a window factory—but that's another story. The bottom line is that no matter how hard I worked or how exhausting or dangerous my work was, it never quite measured up in my mother's mind to picking cotton. She never allowed me into the fraternity. I never got the password. I never made it to the initiation.

One day when she and I were having a discussion about something I thought was funny, but which she did not—a situation I often find myself facing with other folks to this day—I told her I had seen a television interview with Steve Allen wherein he stated that there was humor in everything. To me, this was a brilliant comeback. Steve Allen was, in my mind, something of a Renaissance man of the post-World War II era—a late night television pioneer, musician, comedian, writer, philosopher, conversationalist, and would-be actor—and I quoted him often. In this case, though, the argument failed. Seemingly without concern for logic, Mother simply replied, "Well, if Steven Allen thinks everything is funny, one thing's for sure: he never picked cotton in Texas." Game, set, match. I had no comeback for that. Steven Allen had no comeback for that. But I remember thinking that if I was ever fortunate enough to be president of a prestigious historical organization, I could at least use the line as a title for my presidential paper. And so here we are.

From that discussion with my mother, most likely somewhere in the 1970s, the story moves forward to 1991. She had passed away two years earlier, and I found myself sitting in Temple at the home of her sister, Ganelle Prater Moore, talking over the kitchen table about, once again, picking cotton. I had only recently joined the staff of the Baylor University Institute for Oral History and was planning to develop a research project dealing with life on Texas cotton farms in the Burton area of Washington County. So, I interviewed both Mother's brother and sister for general background. More on the brother later. When my conversation with Aunt Ganelle turned to the inevitable question of which family member picked the most cotton, she told me the oldest sister, Bernice, was by far the best. Then I asked what I thought was the legitimate and logical follow-up question: "Was Mother a good cotton picker?" Aunt Ganelle stared at me for an instant and then started to laugh, and then the laughter intensified, and as she continued to laugh, tears came to her eyes. As she took off her glasses to wipe them away, she said, "Dan, nobody tried harder to avoid picking cotton than your mother."[1]

The truth was out! My mother, the great gatekeeper of the secret order of the cotton picker, in fact spent most of her early field time trying to sneak away from the Bell County cotton patch that would eventually come to identify her own personal work ethic—and mine. While Mother was understandably evasive about that part of her life, she was apparently right about Steve Allen. Nowhere in his autobiography, *Hi Ho, Steverino!*, does he mention spending time in a Texas cotton patch.[2] But, the Allen theory of humor in all circumstances nonetheless held true. As I would find out as I conducted oral histories on cotton farming there was, indeed, humor in the cotton patch. It was, in fact, pervasive, and it percolated through memories time and time again.

That is not to say work in the cotton patch was fun; it was not. It was stoop labor that required field hands to work virtually non-stop from sunup to sundown—or in the farming vernacular, "from can see to can't." The work was tedious, demanding, grueling, mind-numbing, monotonous, and relentless, but it also put food on the table. There were the dangers of an unrelenting sun, of dehydration, poisonous snakes, stinging and biting insects, stinging vegetation, and the poisons used against the boll weevil. And, for those pickers who failed to contribute their fair share to the cause, there was swift punishment from the field supervisor, quite often a mother or grandmother.

But through it all, there was the inevitable humor that somehow evolved from such seeming adversity. Now, to be sure, cotton patch humor is subtle. It is not like the story I heard about a young couple who left the rat race of Houston and traveled up U.S. 59 to Angelina County for the purpose of developing a cotton farm in the Neches River bottoms. According to the story, they worked hard to till up their half-acre and then dutifully planted 500 sterilized cotton balls they bought at a local drugstore. After a couple of weeks they came to the sad conclusion their crop had failed, and believing they had not adequately irrigated their field, they dug the soil once again and planted another 500 balls of cotton. This time they watered faithfully every evening, but the results were the same. No cotton plants; not one. Sensing they needed professional help, they drafted a long letter detailing their predicament and mailed it off to specialists at a well-known agricultural college along the Brazos River. Two weeks later came the following reply: "It's difficult to tell from your letter what the exact nature of the problem could be. We're going to need a soil sample."

No, cotton patch humor is much more subtle—and hopefully funnier—than that apocryphal story. It is borne of the harsh realities and gamblers' trade of agrarian life. I have been collecting farming oral histories for over twenty years now, and wherever I have collected them, from the lower Trinity to the middle Colorado, and from the rocky soils of the Panhandle to the blackland prairies of Washington County, there are the unmistakable and universal rhythms of humor. Without exception, those brought up in the cotton culture have never forgotten the intensity of the labor, the uncertainties of markets and weather, or the common struggles of communities and families, and most have kept all that in a healthy perspective over the years. But they have also preserved the humor that comes from daily events. As Steve Allen so accurately observed, "Nothing is better than the unintended humor of reality."[3]

A good example of a cotton patch humorist was Grover Williams, an African-American farmer who lived outside Burton in Washington County. Williams grew up in the bottomlands of Yegua Creek, a stream known for unpredictable and widespread floods in the days before the impounding of Lake Somerville. The community of his youth was Flat Prairie, a place considered a land of lost cause soil and secondary to the preferred blacklands of the surrounding uplands. Farmers in Flat Prairie were considered by others to be the poorest of the poor, and one German-American farmer I interviewed noted, "When Mr. Jackrabbit went down to Flat Prairie, he packed a sandwich."[4]

Grover Williams was a remarkable man. He grew up in the segregated South but learned to accommodate all kinds of situations. He understood the system and how the system worked, and he made it work for him; it was his chosen method of survival. When he graduated from school, he joined the U.S. Air Force and served in England, then returned to Texas to make a good living in Houston industry before retiring to a farm in Washington County. He had a strong sense of place, both historical and personal.

Williams grew up without his mother, who died when he was a child, the result of a fall from a cotton wagon, and he came to regard his grandmother as his mom. As a young man, he was known as "Bristler," because of his tendency to "bristle up" on occasion like a cur dog. As a young cotton picker, he learned to observe keenly the cultural landscape surrounding him. Take, for example, what I call his story of the educated cousin. The Williams family picked cotton over a wide part of western Washington County, and from the meager funds they collected they systematically set aside money for education, which they saw as a means out of the cotton patch for future generations. But they lacked the money to send all the children to college, so they, in effect, "invested" in Grover Williams' cousin, Ruth Carter, a good student considered likely to succeed. When she graduated from high school, the family sent her off to Tillotson College in Austin. When she returned in the summer, she worked the fields alongside the other family members, although she had fewer responsibilities.

Since Carter represented the family's investment, she received special treatment to protect her from the harsh Texas sun. She wore a long sleeve dress that reached to the ground, gloves that went to her elbows, and a long barrel bonnet that left only a tiny part of her face visible, even when she was looking directly at someone. Her remaining exposed flesh was smeared with an oil-based cream that was black and white, giving her a zebra-like appearance. Thinking back on her unique countenance, Grover

Williams recalled, "I didn't know, during that time, nothing else to compare her with. . . . I thought that's the way college girls looked.⁵

And speaking of bonnets, Williams learned at an early age to read the meaning of their subtle directional nuances like an aviator reads a windsock. His grandmother was the field boss, and she was strict. Unlike others in that capacity, she never allowed her charges to get on their knees to pick cotton. The Williams family always picked standing up. When Grover would protest, crying out, "Mama, my back's hurting," the reply was most often, "Boy you don't have a back, you just got a gristle."⁶ He knew better than to say his gristle was hurting. So, instead, he learned to lock in on the bonnet and follow its direction, even in his peripheral vision. His grandmother was often ahead of him, so when her bonnet would turn away, he would drop to his knees and pick as long as he could. But when the bonnet would swing back in his direction he knew to snap to his feet or face the standard cotton punishment, which was designed to be swift sure, stealthy, and startling—the agricultural equivalent of "shock and awe."

A good field boss knew how to take advantage of the agrarian landscape when meting out punishment to lazy hands, using whatever was available—cotton stalks, dirt clods, green cotton bolls, a hoe handle—to make a point. Williams' brother, Alonzo (nicknamed Snook), was frequently the target, as he never took his work too seriously. He preferred, for example, to chop off the tops of weeds rather than carefully prying them out of the soil So, only a few weeks after the family blitzed a field, chopping cotton as they called it, healthy linear stands of non-cotton vegetation provided unmistakable evidence of the rows where Snook had supposedly toiled. And one time, when he drifted away from the field to rest near a pond and contemplate some far-off vision, a well-aimed green cotton boll caught him sharply on the back of the head, startling him and causing him, as Williams recalled, "to walk water."⁷

Grover Williams had great admiration for his father, and that is clearly evident in his oral histories. Remembering his father's efforts to eradicate the boll weevil, he told:

> We used a Paris green, I think they call it. It's something like arsenic. See, the old man he must have been immune to all that—snakebites and arsenic and poison. See, he didn't have the equipment like the affluent farmers had, you know, where they go in there with sprayers and stuff, whatever. He had to get him a stick, just as wide as the row, you know. The only protection he had on, he had on maybe an old handkerchief

across his mouth. And he had on a little dust bag on each end of that pole. He had to walk, and he'd just shake it over, just walk around and shake it, hoping he'd get enough on there to stop the boll weevil from piercing that boll. It wasn't like a plane coming over with a great big old mist. It was just enough where it didn't do any good.[8]

When Grover Williams and I talked about hog killing time—a special event each fall on farms—he told me about the collecting of hog bladders. As the oldest child, he got to claim the first pig's bladder at slaughter time. This was more significant than it might seem initially. As he described it:

> The bladder is about six inches long and it was green. If you blew into it, it would expand, so you'd blow it and beat it and soon it was bigger than a football. Every time you blew into it, it would stretch some more. You'd keep stretching it, stretch some more, till it got about the size of a beachball. Then you tied it off and you hung it up and let it dry. When it dried, it would be just like paper. Over the hog killing process of that year, you might get three bladders. My other brother would get three, according to how many hog's we'd kill. Everybody had them hanging up—wind blowing just as dry, just like a big piece of thick paper.

And then he elaborated further as to purpose:

> That was for Christmas. I got three pops. See, you got it dry, and Christmas time come—didn't have firecrackers like you got now. You'd put the bladder somewhere and get up on something and you'd jump down on it—POW! Down in Flat Prairie, we didn't have firecrackers and Roman candles. You had to make your own stuff.[9]

With that, I asked what I thought was the appropriate follow-up question: "What did you call those?" "Bladders" was his reply.

Another cotton patch humorist in the Burton area was Eddie Wegner, who grew up in a German-American family. Mr. Wegner had a mechanical and systematic sense about his answers—he liked to explain processes in detail—but he always laced them with a little bit of humor. I interviewed him eleven times, and it seemed like each time there was something interesting going on at the kitchen table where we chose to conduct the interviews, primarily because of Eddie's son, Richard. One time when I was interviewing Eddie Wegner, Richard was breaking down and cleaning a .357 pistol at the table, handing it over to me at times to check it out. Another time he was making sausage. And then another time he was sharpening a Bowie knife he made from a truck spring. I never knew what to expect.

Because Eddie Wegner had such a good memory for details, I was able to interview him about a wide range of aspects of cotton farming. Take, for example, weeds. He described the common vegetative varmints, including cockleburs, grassburs, goatheads, Mexican burrs, white thistles, bull nettle, horse nettle, stinking gourd, and careless weeds. But, even after years away from the cotton patch, he still harbored a special, deep-seated hatred and resentment for Johnson grass, the so-called scourge of the cotton patch. He called it "the plague."

Wegner told about a time when he drove over to the farm of an elderly neighbor: "I drove up and he was pulling Johnson grass, and I said, 'What you doing, Mr. John?' He said, 'I'm trying to take care of this Johnson grass.' I said, 'Don't you know there's hardly any end to that?' He said, 'I well realize that.' I said, 'How long you been fighting it, Mr. John?' He said, 'All my life.'"[10]

Wegner also told of a young man in the Burton community who disliked his older neighbor—just could not stand him for whatever reason. So, each time the young farmer came across some Johnson grass on his land he'd dig up the rhizome and flick it over the fence into the neighbor's field Somehow, this gave him great satisfaction. Well, as the years went by the young man started courting the old farmer's daughter, who grew up to be a lovely woman. The two fell in love and eventually married. Years later, the old farmer died, the couple inherited the land, and the young farmer spent the rest of his life picking Johnson grass out of his field.[11]

Eddie Wegner liked to talk about animals, which he personified—like Mr. Jackrabbit going down into Flat Prairie or Mr. Chickenhawk circling the henhouse. He had an understanding of animals and certainly a respect for them, and it showed in his stories. When he talked about mules, for example, he related how they were hybrids and therefore supposedly sterile. He had personal doubts about that, but he offered as how most people thought the effort to breed mules as, at best, "not a good cause." He recalled how one year his family lost two of their mules in accidents and they needed help fast to keep the fieldwork on schedule. So, Wegner's father borrowed one from his brother-in-law. As he told:

His name was Dick the mule. And Dick was—he was not too long on the working end. To make matters worse, he had been raised in West Texas, where my uncle used to own extensive land, and my uncle was not known to be kind to animals. He worked them pretty hard. And believe it or not, old Dick, when we got him here, he knew exactly what a bedder was—a middle buster plow. That's what he'd put in a lot of hard days with. No matter where a bedder was laying or standing on the place in an idle season, when old Dick walked by it, he would look at it and then kick it with one leg. He knew exactly that was a machine of burden for him.[12]

In reminiscences of pre-tractor cotton patch days, stories of stubborn mules are common, and Wegner provided a classic version. He recalled a neighbor who had a mule that just quit working in the middle of the field one morning—would not budge. The farmer tried the usual trick—beating him with a stick, pulling on the harness, putting sand in his mouth—but nothing worked. So, he found a little dried prairie broom weed at the edge of the field and used it to build a small fire under the mule's belly. The mule would take a few steps forward to avoid the heat but then stop. After a number of small fires and only a few yards to show for the effort, the farmer decided to out-stubborn the stubborn mule. He went to the barn and got a fencepost and drop auger, and he dug a hole next to the mule, set the fencepost, tied the mule up to it and left to do other chores. He left the mule standing out there in the middle of the hot field all day. At sundown, he unhitched the mule, hooked him back to the plow and made him work a few rounds in the field just to show him who was boss. According to Wegner, the balking mule was converted that day.[13]

I ended our discussion of mules by asking Wegner how his family disposed of large animals like mules and horses that died on the farm. He said if they attributed the death to a disease, they either burned or buried the carcasses. If, however, the animals simply died of natural causes, like old age, his family would drag them off to a secluded spot and "the Jones boys would take care of them." That's how he referred to buzzards—the Jones boys.[14]

The Wegners expected every member of the family to work in the field, even women with infant children. Some mothers improvised field care for their children, letting them ride on their cotton sacks, but when the Texas sun was high and hot, they often resorted to other means. Young girls would take turns babysitting under a nearby shade tree, but the Wegners also utilized a "baby box"—a homemade wooden crate on slides, driven to the field by mules, that had a hinged side that could be propped open to provide shade. One of Wegner's earliest memories was of this baby box and the perceived abandonment by his mother. As he recalled, "I would holler, Mama, Mama, Mama, until I couldn't see her chop over the hill anymore. So when she came back, I was elated, of course."[15]

When he became a parent, Wegner took his children to the field as well, even before they could work or walk. Instead of the baby box, though, he kicked the technology up a notch and used a baby buggy with a canopy for shade. One day as he picked cotton near the house, he heard his baby, Robert, gleefully giggling and gurgling and cooing, and he looked up just in time to see a family goat, with the buggy handle firmly in its teeth, gently pushing the buggy down the road.[16]

Wegner also talked about the elites of cotton pickers, those celebrated hands who could out-pick anyone, gathering hundreds of pounds of clean cotton a day. One in particular he remembered was an elderly man named Archie Laws, much in demand by local farmers for his remarkable skills and endurance in the field, and because of his somewhat unique ability to pick two rows of cotton at one time without losing concentration. He would stare straight down the row as he moved along, picking on both sides using peripheral vision and bringing two handfuls of cotton together at the mouth of the sack with a clapping motion. When Wegner asked him about the secret of his success, Laws said, "Well, the best I can explain it to you, one hand must not know what the other hand is doing."[17]

That story contrasts markedly with the personal assessment of Charlie Lincecum, who lived in the Lake Somerville area when I interviewed him. A self-professed poor picker, better suited to hand-digging wells and cisterns than working the patch, Lincecum recalled that even on the best day in the best field he had trouble picking a hundred pounds of cotton. His sister, Bertha, would frequently admonish him to work harder, even meting out justice by whipping him with an uprooted cotton plant, bolls and all, right there in the field. As an adult hand, Lincecum recalled one particular incident where, as he weighed his cotton sack at the end of the day, the farmer to whom he had hired out observed, "You must have just come down here to eat."[18]

One last comment about Eddie Wegner: he is unfortunately no longer with us, but I have great memories of his love for life. He always seemed genuinely happy to see me when we would visit, and he always greeted me with a great smile. He thoroughly enjoyed sharing cotton patch stories with me. When I last saw him several years ago, long after our sessions ended, he said, "You know, it's good you interviewed me when you did. I seem to be getting freckle-minded these days." An interesting description of what would later be clinically diagnosed as Alzheimer's disease.[19]

Now, stepping outside the boundaries of East Texas, let me tell you about an interviewee from Turkey in Hall County, not far from Amarillo. That was the boyhood home of Curtis Tunnell, the first State Archeologist of Texas, later executive director of the Texas Historical Commission, and my public history mentor in matters related to historic preservation, oral history, and traveling Texas. I conducted more than fifty interviews with Tunnell, and his memories of life on a West Texas farm were remarkably clear and poignant. He had an ability—a gift, really—to recall the past with incredibly beautiful prose, in both spoken memory and verse, that to me evoked an artist's view, as in this written description of his childhood landscape:

> Turkey was a beautiful place for a boy to grow up in the years before World War II. My earliest memories are of looking toward the west and seeing the sculptured purple silhouette of the Caprock. This rugged escarpment of the plains beckoned steadily, from the twin Quitaque Peaks on the south to Eagles Point on the north. This vista always made my mind take flight. . . .I never knew anything drab or monotonous.[20]

Tunnell was, by the local societal standards, a city boy. He grew up in the town of Turkey, but his parents worked on area farms as what he called "hoe hands." He said he preferred that term to "hoers," which he felt did not sound as distinguished. Tunnell's father and grandfather worked in the Turkey gins and compress, and other members of the family helped raise extra money by hiring out for picking and chopping. The Tunnell children worked across the area far and wide, often utilizing the small train known locally as the doodlebug to reach nearby farms, including those of their extended family. One such farm was near the Edgin spur, the site of a dispersed community called Grey Mule, now only a ghost town on the High Plains. Today, you can reach the site of the settlement by means of a Texas Parks and Wildlife hiking and equestrian trail that utilizes the old rail bed, the route of the doodlebug. Here is Tunnell's description of one particular time when they had to catch the train at Grey Mule:

> You had to flag the train. In those days, if anybody along the track wanted to go somewhere, they'd just go out and flag the doodlebug, and the doodlebug would stop. One time we

went out, and cousin Nora Dale was with us. So, the doodlebug had come down off the plains and was coming real fast down the track. Oh, we all began to holler that it looked like the train wasn't going to stop, even though we were there beside the track. So, Nora Dale had on a red half-slip. She stepped out of that red half-slip, and she waved that red half-slip. The train came to a screeching halt.[21]

Tunnell's description of Turkey as a typical High Plains cotton town in the 1940s is rich. As he recalled:

> One thing that is interesting about a cotton town is that during the ginning season, they were burning burrs at all five of the gins. We lived a block northeast of one gin, and there was always a southwest wind. The smell of those burning burrs permeated the whole countryside. . . . It has a very distinctive smell. I smelled it from my earliest days when I was right there a block from those cotton gins. I can't describe what it smells like, but it's like dry weeds or something. It's not an unpleasant smell to me. When Mama would hang the clothes out to dry, the smoke would be coming, and they'd get smoked in that. I always thought that fresh sheets and fresh clothes, fresh shirts, were supposed to smell like cotton smoke.[22]

Let me conclude with another of those cotton patch characters, my mother's brother, Thomas Francis Prater, Jr.—known as T.F. to the family. This brings us back to the blackland prairie of Bell County, where the paper began. T.F. Prater had a remarkable, lifelong ability of surrounding himself with other interesting characters, and he had a good memory for their stories. He remembered little details that made people sound funny, like "one of the McKee boys," a neighbor who played his clarinet at night in the cotton patch. On more than one occasion, it seems, the McKee boy's moonlight serenade coaxed coyotes right in upon him.[23] And then there was another neighbor who made peach brandy in a remote section of the Prater land. The fermented pulp he left behind on the ground attracted animals, including the Prater hogs, that were eventually blitzed, running all over the farm, squealing and carrying on.[24]

Prater had a good sense of family history as well, and he recalled how my grandmother, Florence Nott Prater, a devout Southern Baptist, nevertheless kept a small bottle of whiskey handy for "medicinal purposes." When she administered some to her sick children, she was careful to pour a little in a saucer and light it to burn off the alcohol, evidently making it okay for Baptist consumption. My grandfather, on the other hand, was not as theologically dogmatic as his wife, although he was apparently health conscious, so he generally took his medicine alone in the barn, without a saucer or a match, more in the manner of the Episcopalians.[25]

According to Prater, his father, a somewhat serious man who had a strong set of personal rules—not to be confused with stubbornness—insisted on biscuits to accompany his breakfast every morning. It was tradition, and my grandfather rarely messed with tradition. My grandmother faithfully complied, rising early each day to make scratch biscuits, but one day, in some unexplainable moment of independent creativity, she changed the routine and made toast. That defiance angered my grandfather so much that, according to his son, "He didn't go and even sit down to eat." He went to the field because he would rather do that than eat a piece of light bread.[26]

In his oral memoirs, Prater spoke of how farmers often had long-held allegiances to particular product lines—ties that could be transgenerational. His father was, for example, a Farmall tractor man, although there was a brief, unexplained, and ultimately disappointing, dalliance with the Fordson line. But according to my uncle, "Old man Cross" (a neighbor) was a McCormick Deering man—International Harvester. His tractor was McCormick Deering, his implements were all McCormick Deering, his thrasher was McCormick Deering, and he added, "I heard a fellow say one time, Mr. Cross's mules is [sic] McCormick Deering."[27]

I have to add just one more story about my grandfather and my uncle. It has only a tangential, political connection with the cotton patch, but it speaks also to his strongly-held traditions. Granddaddy Prater was on his deathbed in the Santa Fe Hospital in Temple during the early 1970s. He had laid there quiet and almost motionless for days, and we knew the end was near. But as news of Richard Nixon and some related Watergate matter came on the television in his room, he suddenly mumbled something. My uncle went to his side, leaned down and said, "What's that, Daddy?" A moment of silence and then Granddaddy said, "They ought to knock him in the head." The old farmer was until the very end a New Deal Democrat.[28]

So, was there, in fact, humor in the cotton patch? Was my cotton-picking mother right, or does Steve Allen's axiom of comedy prevail? Like most questions in history, I guess, it comes down to matters of context, perspective, and interpretation. In a sense, though, it also comes down to the continually changing cultural landscape. How do we make sense of such a distinct historical era, with humor or otherwise, when so many of the landmarks, personal and otherwise, are gone? Cotton no longer grows around Burton, for example. It has, in effect, gone west and south to larger farm operations, and cattle now roam the former fields of the Williams and Wegner families. Many early Panhandle gins and compresses, as well as the small family farms where the Tunnells toiled, have given way to large agri-business concerns, and the settlement of Grey Mule is only a memory along a trail. The Prater farm in Bell County is long gone as well, although if you know where to look you can detect the refurbished farmhouse in the Marland Woods subdivision of Temple, down the road from the massive Scott and White Hospital campus. And if you are a golfer, you can drive your cart to the exact site of the Utley farmhouse near Salado and tee off on the par four 18th hole at Mill Creek Golf Course, not far from where my grandfather died working his hardscrabble land for the sake of cotton and family and prosperity.

In the vernacular of the cotton patch, farmers often spoke of "scrappin' cotton," the end of the season process of going back over the field after the primary picking to harvest the few threads—the so-called "goose tails"—that remained in most bolls. It was a limited harvest to be sure, but it could produce additional funds, and in such a society, all funds were helpful and genuinely appreciated. In a sense, historians today are likewise challenged to scrap the cotton. The crop was such an integral part of our culture for so long, there will always be those who study its sweeping impact, from economics, labor, and the environment to agriculture, class struggle, and sociology. But to me, it always comes back to a set of fingers reaching down deep into a cotton boll, carefully maneuvering around the razor-sharp burrs, securing the center and twisting it slightly but deliberately—and maybe without the right hand knowing what the left hand is doing—carefully picking out the thin white threads for whatever reason. There was an inherent promise in the process. It was the human side of the cotton equation, and with that humanity as the primary focus, we can still discover and analyze all of its historical facets—maybe even, if we listen closely—the humor.

NOTES

1. Personal recollection of the author.

2. Steve Allen, *Hi-Ho, Steverino! My Adventures in the Wonderful Wacky World of TV*. Fort Lee, NJ: Barricade Books, 1992.

3. Quote publicly attributed to Steve Allen; exact source unknown.

4. Eddie Wegner, Burton, Texas, oral history interview with Dan K. Utley, Baylor University Institute for Oral History, January 22, 1992. Comment about Flat Prairie made off tape.

5. Grover Williams, Burton, Texas, oral history interview with Dan K. Utley, Baylor University Institute for Oral History, November 25, 1991.

6. Ibid.

7. Grover Williams, oral history interview with Dan K. Utley, Baylor University Institute for Oral History, May 22, 1992.

8. Williams, November 25, 1991.

9. Grover Williams, oral history interview with Dan K. Utley, Baylor University Institute for Oral History, May 8, 1992.

10. Eddie Wegner, oral history interview with Dan K. Utley, Baylor University Institute for Oral History, March 18, 1992.

11. Ibid; story told off tape; personal recollection of the author.

12. Eddie Wegner, oral history interview with Dan K. Utley, Baylor University Institute for Oral History, February 20, 1992.

13. Eddie Wegner, oral history interview with Dan K. Utley, public historian, September 9, 1994. Tapes deposited with the Baylor University Institute for Oral History.

14. Wegner, February 20, 1992.

15. Wegner, March 18, 1992.

16. Wegner, February 20, 1992.

17. Eddie Wegner, oral history interview with Dan K. Utley, public historian, September 16, 1994. Tapes deposited with the Baylor University Institute for Oral History.

18. Charlie Lincecum, Lee County, Texas, oral history interview with Dan K. Utley, Baylor University Institute for Oral History, August 28, 1992.

19. Personal recollection of the author.

20. Personal writings of Curtis D. Tunnell, October 1999. Papers in the possession of Dan K. Utley.

21. Curtis D. Tunnell, Austin, Texas, oral history interview with Dan K. Utley, public historian, January 27, 1995. Tapes and transcripts in possession of the Texas Historical Commission; excerpted transcripts in possession of the Texas Parks and Wildlife Department.

22. Curtis D. Tunnell, oral history interview with Dan K. Utley.

23. Thomas Francis Prater, Jr., Livingston, Texas, oral history interview with Dan K. Utley, Baylor University Institute for Oral History, June 15, 1993.

24. Ibid.

25. Ibid.

26. Ibid.

27. Thomas Francis Prater, Jr., oral history interview with Dan K. Utley, Baylor University Institute for Oral History, June 16, 1993.

28. Ibid; personal recollection of the author.

Journey from Tampa to Dallas to Nacogdoches

Theodore Lawe

I would like to thank the members of the East Texas Historical Association for the opportunity to serve as president for this past year. I am pleased with the growth of the association in terms of membership, revenues, and staff leadership. From a personal point of view, my being president of the association has brought additional recognition to the A. C. McMillan African American Museum in Emory. A case in point: Dr. Light Cummins of Austin College in Sherman, who the governor designated as the State Historian, recently visited the museum and gave us an unqualified positive review. We thank him for his visit and his blog report, which so many read. Another case in point is that I received the Trailblazer Award from the South Dallas Business and Professional Women's Club, and I thank Scott Sosebee for being part of the crowd in attendance at that ceremony.

As I was sitting here at the head table, I told my wife Gwen that this reminds me of the time when I gave my first major speech in Detroit. The person in charge told me that since I was a recent appointee I could take as long as I needed to express myself. I talked for approximately forty-five minutes. Then I said, "In conclusion," and I talked for approximately another thirty minutes, and then I said, "I want to leave with you one thought," and I talked for another twenty minutes. The difficulty in this kind of a speech is where to start. Although Scott Sosebee told me I could take as long as I like, I will be prudent in time, because my wife gave me a second watch for time control.

On a more serious note, the journey from Tampa to Dallas to Nacogdoches is 1,268 miles. I have seen many social changes in all aspects of American life and in East Texas, where I have spent more than thirty-five years. Looking back at my personal experiences that influenced my growth and development, I think of my summer jobs with Fahnestock and Company, a Wall Street brokerage firm, where I served as a runner. Back in those pre-computer days, we physically transported stock certificates. Another early experience that influenced my growth and development was the summer of 1964, when I was employed under the Foreign Affairs Scholars Program with the Agency for International Development (AID) in the U.S. State Department in Washington, DC.

As has been stated in the introduction, I am a graduate of

Bethune-Cookman University, where I served as president of the Student Government Association in my senior year. I earned, with honors, a bachelor's degree in political science with a minor in history. After Bethune-Cookman, I enrolled in the Atlanta University graduate school and earned an MA in history, and wrote a thesis entitled, "Black Reconstruction in Georgia: Contributions of Henry McNeal Turner." He was the first African American chaplain in the army and later served in the Georgia Legislature. He was a strong voice for freedom and civil rights.

As I graduated from Atlanta University, I had nine job offers (Humble Oil Company/American Can Company/Reynolds Aluminum Company). This was in 1966 at the height of African Americans employment in nontraditional jobs. I accepted a position as a management assistant with the Tennessee Valley Authority (TVA) headquartered in Knoxville. While working with TVA, I enrolled at the University of Tennessee and earned an MA in urban and regional planning. After graduating from UT and working with TVA, I accepted a position as director of research with a small management and consulting firm and traveled extensively in the northeast: New Haven, Connecticut; New London, Connecticut; Philadelphia, Pennsylvania; and Atlantic City, New Jersey. During that time, I spent one summer studying at Yale University.

In 1970, I accepted the position as executive assistant to the mayor of Detroit, Michigan. The person who introduced me to Mayor Roman S. Gribbs was Frank Logue, the mayor of New Haven. I spent four years in Detroit, and among my areas of responsibility were serving as liaison to the Department of Parks and Recreation, the Mayor's Committee for Human Resources Development, public libraries, and the Art Institute. Additionally, I helped in organizing and managing the Neighborhood City Halls Program (still in existence today), and I worked with Ralph Abernathy and the Southern Christian Leadership Conference to resolve the garbage workers' strike. I also attended Wayne State University's doctoral program and finished all requirements except my dissertation. Other things that I remember from the Detroit experience include the firing of the police chief, fixing parking tickets, John Mays' conversation, and Hubert Humphrey's visit to the city.

Another call from Frank Logue in 1974 connected me to the city manager of Dallas, George Schraeder. I served as assistant city manager from 1974 to 1979, and that was the first time an African American served in that capacity for the city. In Dallas, my basic responsibilities included handling all federal money under general revenue sharing and categorically funded programs, organizing the Office of Human development and Environmental Health, and developing the strategy for organizing the Office of Economic Development, which became the robust Department of Economic Development with a dynamic director. My recollections from that position were meeting A. Maceo Smith, attending city council meetings in Alex Bickley's office, and being on a radio program with George Gallop. Additional areas of reflection involved teaching four years as an adjunct professor in the Public Administration Program, initiating contracts with several nonprofit organizations (OIC, Dallas Urban League, Operation SER), traveling to the Republic of China in 1979 with the State Department, and writing the book *How to Secure and Manage Federal Funds*.

In 1979, I left Dallas City Hall and started my journey as an entrepreneur by organizing Metroplex Research and Development Consultants (MRDC). I initially had contracts with the Xerox Corporation and the 1982 World's Fair in Knoxville. I later secured contracts with the TVA, Dallas Independent School District, DFW International Airport Board, Chrysler Corporation, and Waste Management. In the consulting capacity, I traveled sixty percent of my time in Kentucky, Alabama, Tennessee, Mississippi, Georgia, and Washington, DC. In 1980, I bought a struggling company called State Cab Company and later developed it into a fleet of 350 vehicles, with five million dollars in annual revenue. In 1988, I became a part of a joint venture called Accommodations, Inc., and operated several concessions at DFW Airport, Reunion Arena, Dallas Convention Center, and Dallas Love Field. In 1991, I organized Maxwell Enterprises Limited and went back into the consulting business with such clients as the City of Dallas and Dallas County. We conducted several studies, including a benchmark study for community grant funds. In 1998, I organized Maxwell Land Development Company, Inc. and focused on real estate investments.

In 2000, Gwen and I founded the A.C. McMillan African American Museum in Emory. Prior to opening the museum, in the summer of 1999, we visited several African American heritage venues in Tennessee, Virginia, South Carolina, North Carolina, Georgia, Alabama, Louisiana, and Washington, DC. Other items of interest included finding a space and preparing for the museum, starting collections, recruiting volunteers, establishing collaborative relationships, and joining the Texas Association of Museums.

In 2001, we joined the East Texas Historical Association. Since then, we have presented in several workshops and served on the board in several capacities. A call from Cary Wintz, chair of the nominating committee, led to my being elected second vice president and later first vice president, and now president of the association.

There are many unexplored areas for historical researchers on the African American experience in East Texas. Among them are the rising black middle class and its origin and development, and the African American pioneers, who in many cases did not participate directly in the Civil Rights Movement but were among the first to serve in various capacities.

As I step down from the presidency of the East Texas Historical Association, I leave the following challenges to those members and leaders who will follow. We need to recruit more members from underserved groups, such as African Americans, Hispanics, Native Americans, and Asians. We need to involve more cultural institutions in the activities of the association, while diversifying all committees, including the editorial board.

Let me just close by saying, the journey from Tampa to Dallas to Nacogdoches—my journey—has been a good ride.

A River Creeps Through It

Milton S. Jordan

Along the banks of a slough in West Virginia, not East Texas, an American poet considered, "A little cloud of inaudible gnats, In a shaft of morning sunlight." He compared that cloud to the shadows of a middle-aged catfish in the shallows of the slough. The poet, Franz Wright, then asked:

God, what is the meaning of
This minute.
Tell me; I ask you.
I have already been here
Forever, he replies,
And think I'm going to stay.[1]

I cannot speak to the eternal presence of the divine along the sloughs or backwaters of our East Texas rivers. If we are searching for something real, though, something at least almost permanent, we could not find a better place to look than along these rivers and the sand ridges that separate them. Rivers write their own dissertations along their banks and under the roots of trees upon them. In East Texas, we hear them read in low gurgles or occasional rushes through the narrows. We see a few visual aids still present in the pine forests and on the sandy meadows.

I am enough of an incarnationist to think that God chooses to show up in all sorts of worldly places. In one of my sources, I learned that God came to dwell along a Middle Eastern river from which my family takes its name. Richard Donovan, in his book, *Paddling the Wild Neches*, reminded me of an East Texas prophetic writer, Archer Fullingim of the *Kountze News*.[2] Fullingim once wrote in his column, "Both Barrels," "I am sure the Holy Spirit lives in the bottom lands along the Neches River in East Texas."[3] Another of our prophetic writers, Fullingim's contemporary, Roy Bedichek, used a slightly different image to describe his experience walking through a stand of uncut first growth timber along the Neches. It was, he wrote, "An island of life in the midst of a weary land."[4]

The Neches was my father's river. He lived much of his life along it from Edgewood near its head to Beaumont and Port Neches at its mouth, and Jasper and Keltys in between. My earliest memories are of a small town in Camp County along Cypress Creek. When it gets closer to Louisiana, they call the Cypress a bayou. It empties into Caddo Lake. We lived in Pittsburg, up at the northern end of East Texas, for seven years. In the midst of elementary school, we moved three hundred miles south and lived for ten years along Goose Creek in a town once named for that sluggish stream. I have always been fascinated by these creeks and rivers around us: the San Jacinto and the Trinity, Buffalo Bayou and Attoyac Bayou. Even in elementary school, it dawned on me how significant the confluence of Buffalo Bayou with the San Jacinto was to the battle fought on those plains and the bogs around them. Our history is inseparable from our geography, and our geography is determined by the rivers that creep through it.

Wherever you are in East Texas geography, a river is creeping along—or damned—very near your place. If not a river, then a creek or a bayou is within easy reach. The preservation and restoration of these streams is essential to the vitality of our region. And, the identification and preservation of the scenes and stories along them is essential to maintaining our historic and cultural heritage. The scenes and the stories of our ancestors, their friends—and their enemies—keep disappearing in the face of rapid development, poorly thought through.

Survey work at archaeological sites now inundated by Lake Wright Patman, for example, identified numerous villages occupied along the Sulphur River before major European contact with the native folks there. These sites are no longer available to us. In an interview with the archaeologist, Curtis Tunnell, Dan K. Utley asked how much archaeology he thought he salvaged from McGee Bend on the Angelina before that dam went in. "Probably just a fraction of one percent," Curtis said. "There must have been many hundreds or several thousand sites in that area. We only worked in a dozen or so and only took samples out of those. . . . We were getting an extremely small sample out of all those sites."[5] Those sites are now under water or silt.

Cultural resource professionals like Curtis Tunnell are often employed to conduct mitigation research before valuable historic evidence is completely destroyed by public highway or dam construction. More often than not, private development projects make little or no effort to salvage any such historic evidence. Ever larger reservoirs to provide water for expanding urban areas come with a price. Quarter- or half-mile-wide super freeways between those areas and multi-acre asphalt parking lots in suburbs around them are at least as costly. Beyond the economic and environmental cost-benefit balance, we especially are concerned with the great loss of archaeological, cultural and historic resources and records.

Surely, we share the concerns of many for the environmental values lost to such development projects. Our concern, though, our primary concern, is with the historic and cultural records and resources we are losing. The rivers of East Texas attracted folks to them long before any written records were kept. The rivers provided a relative ease of travel and nourished life in the dense forest. Here along these rivers then are the scenes and stories of countless generations who have traveled on them and settled between them. We are the ones to identify and preserve those scenes. We are the ones to research and tell those stories.

The European segment of those stories likely begins with Luis Moscoso, who inherited the ragged remains of the DeSoto expedition. According to Jim Bruseth and Nancy Kenmotsu, in their essay, "From Naguatex to the River Daycao," Moscoso came south from the Great Bend of the Red River in the summer of 1542. He may well have crossed the Neches just southwest of here in his unsuccessful effort to reach New Spain. The local folks must have thought this an odd group of travelers. Some were riding strange large animals and dressed in fancy armored outfits; most were shuffling along draped in rags. With the help of archaeologists like Bruseth and Kenmotsu, we learn that even before the arrival of these hopelessly lost Spaniards, people along these streams were encountering strange travelers.[6]

Certainly in the four hundred and fifty years since then, a remarkably diverse bunch of people have wandered through and settled in East Texas. Scattered all around us, everywhere from the Sulphur and the Cypress to Sabine Lake and Trinity Bay, are the cultural, historic and social records and resources of these peoples, their lives, and the communities they established. We are letting way too many of these records and resources slip away, not only because they disappear under various development projects, but more important for us, because we are not as active as we could be in searching out and telling their stories. I certainly regret my own failures to go with my father and later with my oldest sister to check out scenes and stories they knew well along the Neches.

In their collection, *Making East Texas, East Texas*, editors Bruce Glasrud and Archie McDonald remind us that East Texas is more than a compass reference.[7] We do not say eastern Texas. This is a region of a state, to be sure, but it is a state of mind as well, they tell us. I take that to mean that the scenes and stories of how and where we lived with one another are essential to understanding what makes East Texas, East Texas today. When we are looking for some of those things almost permanent, look for places where, long after Moscoso, other Europeans settled the red hills and prairies along the Neches and our other streams. Search for the stories of the slaves and servants who came with them. Think of the local peoples native to this area and those driven here by European settlement elsewhere who lived around and among them. Most of their stories still wait for someone—maybe one of us—to tell them.

In his book, *Texas Riverman,* William Seale tells one of these stories. Capt. Andrew Smyth traveled on the Neches and the Angelina from early republic days to the end of Reconstruction. In his preface to the new edition of the book, Seale tells us that in those days, "The riverways of East Texas provided a freedom of movement that the muddy, stump scattered frontier roadways could not provide."[8] Stories of rivermen and steamboaters and their families still wait to be told from Smithport to Bevilport to Port Neches.

Thad Sitton and Jim Conrad tell us of another group of East Texans in their book *Freedom Colonies: Independent Black Texans in the Time of Jim Crow.* They identify nearly three hundred of these freedom colonies along the river bottoms of East Texas and up on the sand ridges between the creeks. At the turn of the last century, most Texas African-American landowners lived in these formal or less formal communities of black farmers and stockmen scattered across the eastern half of Texas.[9] These were people who, by fact and by law, were marginalized and shut out of opportunities open to many of their neighbors. Yet, in the face of nearly impossible conditions, they established something of permanent value. Residents of these communities built homes, commercial and agricultural enterprises, and churches and schools often housed in the same buildings. Thanks to our friends O.L. Davis, Gwen Lawe, and Ted Lawe, and others, we know that many of these communities later built new schools with the help of the Rosenwald Fund. Julius Rosenwald began funding the building of schools for African Americans in the rural South at the end of World War I. In the next fifteen years, more than five hundred of those schools were built in Texas, more than half of those in our East Texas area. Most of their stories are yet to be told.[10]

Jonathan Gerland, in a presentation at an earlier association meeting, told us of another group of people, marginalized and shut out of most opportunities. Though they did not share fully in the rewards, crews of Mexican Americans provided labor on the rail lines and in the forests that were essential to the early East Texas timber industry.[11] In their online digital project at Sam Houston State University, "Democracy and Diversity in Walker County," Rosanne Barker, Jeff Littlejon, Bernadette Pruitt and others tell us several such stories like that of Boettcher's Mill. At the beginning of the twentieth century, Baldwin Boettcher, an immigrant from Germany, established a sawmill in Montgomery County.

When harvestable timber in that area gave out, his son Ed Boettcher reestablished the mill in Walker County. The community of Boettcher's Mill, reconstructed just outside Huntsville, housed the mill workers and their families. A significant number of these families were Mexican immigrants. The community also housed African American and Anglo American workers and their families.[12]

These are a few stories of people who, against very difficult odds, established lives and communities that offer us glimpses, at least, of near permanent value. These are stories of people who make East Texas, East Texas. We can hope their stories direct our attention to the hundreds of scenes and stories like them waiting for East Texas historians to identify and to tell. Surely, we are grateful that battle sites like the plains of San Jacinto are preserved. We appreciate the recording and telling of stories of military engagements and their strategies and tactics. The stories of where we fought with one another, though, are usually well preserved. The stories of how we fought with one another are oft retold.

Scenes and stories of where and how we lived with one another are often neglected. Freedom colonies like Fodice in Houston County, or workers' communities like Boettcher's Mill in Walker County, more often disappear and take their stories with them. We might be about our business as historians—professional and amateur—finding and preserving these sites and recording and telling these stories. Ask yourself what songs the people sang. Find out who made the music. Look for those places where sharing and cooperation were the tactics and where the people's strategy was to create or recreate community. Look for those places. Tell those stories.

Let me paraphrase an old Yiddish proverb from a collection called *Perek*. It is not up to us to complete the task, but neither are we free to desist from it.[13]

NOTES

1. Franz Wright, "The Catfish" in his collection *Wheeling Motel*, New York, Knopf, 2009. p. 72.

2. Richard Donovan, *Paddling the Wild Neches*, College Station, Texas A&M University Press, 2006, p. 3.

3. Archer Fullingim, *A Country Editor's View of Life*, edited by Roy Hamric, Austin, Heidelberg Publishers, 1975.

4. Roy Bedichek, *Adventures with a Texas Naturalist*, New York, Doubleday, 1947, p. 67.

5. Curtis Tunnell, Oral History interview with Dan K. Utley, March 6, 2000, Texas Historical Commission.

6. Jim Bruseth and Nancy Kenmotsu, "From Naguatex to the River Daycao: The Route of the Hernando DeSoto Expedition through Texas," in *North American Archaeologist*, Vol. 14 (3) pp. 199-225, 1993.

7. Bruce A. Glasrud and Archie P. McDonald, editors, *Making East Texas, East Texas: Selections from the East Texas Historical Journal*, East Texas Historical Association, 2009, p. 6.

8. William Seale, *Texas Riverman: The Life and Times of Captain Andrew Smyth*, 2nd edition, Temple, Ink Brush Press, 2009, Preface. Originally published by University of Texas Press, 1966.

9. Thad Sitton and James H. Conrad, *Freedom Colonies: Independent Black Texans in the Time of Jim Crow*, Austin, University of Texas Press, 2005,

10. James Conrad and Theodore M. Lawe. "Preserving Rosenwald Schools in East Texas: The Sand Flat and Richland School Project," in the *East Texas Historical Journal*, Vol. 43 (2) 2005, pp. 50-57.

11. Jonathan Gerland, "Working on the Neches Valley Route: A History of the Texas South-Eastern Railroad." A paper presented to the East Texas Historical Association, Nacogdoches, September 28, 2001.

12. Jeff Littlejohn et al, "Democracy and Diversity in Walker County." Online project at Sam Houston State University, http//www.studythepast.com.

13. Aaron Lansky, *Outwitting History: The Amazing Adventures of a Man Who Rescued a Million Yiddish Books*, Chapel Hill, Algonquin Books, 2005, p. 300.

Is Our Collective Memory Folklore or History?

Tom Crum

Several years ago, Odessa was competing with other West Texas cities for a state college. Advocates for each city appeared before the State College Coordinating Board. The late Warren Burnett, a competent trial lawyer from Odessa, represented that city. After Mr. Burnett's presentation, the chairman of the board asked him if he honestly believed there was justification for a four-year college in Odessa. Mr. Burnett replied, "Mr. Chairman, there is enough ignorance in Odessa to justify an eight-year college." Odessa got the college.

I never had the opportunity to meet Mr. Burnett, but if he is like most of us lawyers, he was well qualified to speak on the subject of ignorance. However, since ignorance is nothing more than a lack of knowledge, we are all ignorant, just in different subjects. I don't consider myself an expert when it comes to knowledge, but as to the vast field of ignorance, well to be honest, I feel that I am quite accomplished in that field. I might add, that feeling is shared by all of my former teachers.

There are numerous ways in which we acquire knowledge. Just to name a few, we can acquire it through our experiences and observations, by reading books and articles, watching educational programs on television, visiting educational and cultural sites, attending lectures or other informative gatherings, or by paying attention in class, something that many of us found difficult when the seating chart placed a potential homecoming queen directly between us, the teacher, and the blackboard. After all, as the Rick Trevino song asks, "How were we expected to get an education, sitting right behind Bobby Ann Mason?"

We become acquainted with knowledge of historical events through these and other means. If the sources of our knowledge of historical events are those shared by most of our fellow citizens, then our and their remembrance of these events will form what historians refer to as collective memory. Collective memory has been defined as a memory or memories shared or recollected by a group, as a community or culture—any collection of memories passed from one generation to the next, the collection of memories shared by a common culture.

Francis Abernethy, the longtime executive secretary and editor of the Texas Folklore Society, defines folklore as "the traditional knowledge of a culture." Tradition means the handing down of statements, beliefs, legends, customs, information, and so on, from generation to generation. Consequently, as to historical knowledge, I find no difference between what historians refer to as collective memory and what folklorists refer to as folklore, and I suspect historians came up with the term "collective memory" because they were afraid of the word folklore, and they wanted to protect and cover their reputations, or whatever.

I know we have some historians and folklorists in this group, and although I am neither one, I do have friends in both camps. If you look around, you will be able to identify the folklorists. They are the ones who look smug and content. That is because they know that unless they are foolish enough to write about the history of folklore, it is impossible for them to make a mistake. They know that no one will ever accuse them of getting their facts wrong or of writing politically correct folklore and, of course, there is no such thing as revisionist folklore. If someone ever accused a folklorist of making a mistake, all the folklorist has to say is, "that's the way I heard it," and he or she is off the hook and waiting for an apology. Sadly, it is not the same for historians; they are seldom off the hook and never receive apologies. It is enough to make even folklorists sympathetic toward historians, and I am sure the more charitable ones are. I personally have never witnessed any concern on their part, but that may say more about the company I keep than folklorists as a group.

There is a great deal of correct history in folklore. This history provides the basis for many of folklore's most entertaining accounts. If folklore and collective memory are the same, then it follows that there is a great deal of correct history in our collective memory. However, whereas folklore does not claim or pretend that what it presents as to a particular event is true and factual, our collective memory does make such claims and pretensions. It was the folklorist, J. Frank Dobie, who stated something to the effect that if something didn't happen a certain way, it should have. Folklore can get away with such statements, history cannot. Regrettably, much of what we consider to be the history of an event is nothing more than folklore in disguise. Folklore is not all fun and games. It does perform important services. It often aids us in understanding a culture. Louise Cowan tells us, "One discerns a society's vision of the nature and destiny of humanity through its legendary material, its folklore, its fairytales." Dobie also advised us that an anecdote of doubtful historicity might reveal more about a man or people than a book full of facts.

Historians and folklorists often use the same sources for their accounts. One example is personal accounts or remembrances. Whereas, folklorists depend heavily on these, historians also make frequent use of them. While the folklorist is not concerned with the accuracy of the account or what is remembered, but only that it makes a good story, the historian vouches for the accuracy of the account or what is remembered. This often causes problems for the historian. People not only forget, they lie. Since none of these personal accounts is subject to cross-examination, perhaps in evaluating them the historian should take advantage of the rules of evidence that we use in our legal system. If the historian uses the account to prove, as we lawyers say, the truth of the matter asserted, it is not subject to cross-examination, it is hearsay. Although hearsay evidence is admissible under certain circumstances, generally it is excluded as being unreliable. As the bluegrass song "Daddy Played the Banjo" warns us, "Memories of what never was become the good old days," and that, of course, although true, presents another recurring problem with recorded memories and hearsay. That is, many such memories contain self-serving statements that would be inadmissible and omit statements against interest, which would be admissible. In any event, historians need to use caution when relying on personal accounts or interviews. The majority of those who give these accounts and interviews are older people. After all, they have had more experiences and therefore have more to tell us about past events. Let's face it, we don't send Barbara Walters to interview these people or gather their accounts. We send people who will get along with them, and that means people who will not ask any hard questions. The last thing we old people want is someone asking hard questions, or for that matter any questions. We just want to talk. I suspect historians sit around and tell each other that someone should go and interview old so and so before it's too late. They don't say it, but they all know what that means. If I had an honest occupation, like selling life insurance, I wouldn't sell to anyone who was going to be interviewed by one of these historians. The second question I would ask a potential customer—that is right after I asked, "How are you feeling?"—would be, "Has anyone asked you for an interview?"

The danger of relying too much on personal accounts and remembrances and other questionable sources can be a problem for a historian. However, we lay people have enough problems of our own in dealing with our collective memory to spend much time worrying about and feeling sorry for historians.

By not giving the two most important words in the definition of collective memory the respect they deserve, we have caused our own problems. Those words are, "a culture." Since there are many different cultures in any society, there are often many different stories or accounts passed on as traditional knowledge of any one historical event. As folklore, all of these are of equal value. However, although each of them may have some nodding acquaintance with the actual facts of the event, none of them may be factually true. The southern whites' traditional knowledge of slavery, the antebellum South and Reconstruction as passed on to them by their cultural ancestors may be very different from the traditional knowledge of the same subjects that is passed on to the descendants of slaves by their cultural ancestors. The collective memories of different cultures in any society may be, and often are, very different. However, it is the collective memory of the dominant culture in any society that forms or greatly influences the collective memory of all cultures in that society, especially as to events that do not pertain to a particular non-dominant culture. When someone writes a historical account of an event that runs counter to the dominant culture's collective memory, many in that culture will accuse the author of being a historical revisionist and possibly also of writing politically correct history. They do not mean for either of these descriptions to be taken as a compliment. What they are saying is that someone has messed with their history and they don't like it. The emphasis is on "their."

"The" history of an event can never be written; the best we can hope for is "a" history of the event. When a historian writes a history of an event that has previously been covered in other histories, he or she has either discovered some new information concerning the event, or using already discovered information has evaluated that information differently than has been done before. There is nothing wrong with this, since research and evaluation of facts are part of the job description of the historian. If it were otherwise, there would never be any need for another book covering the Civil War, the Texas Rangers, the frontier, and thousands of other subjects that have been previously covered in earlier histories. To most anti-revisionists that would probably be just fine. Of course, since it would put them out of business, there are no historians in the anti-revisionist camp, and since folklorists see nothing wrong with revision, especially if it makes the story better, they also camp elsewhere.

Now, don't make the mistake of thinking that anti-revisionists think all newly written accounts that question some aspect of their collective memory is revisionist or politically correct history. If the new history reinforces what their collective memory perceives to be some positive aspect of their culture, or places one of their heroes or their culture in a more favorable light, or reinforces what their collective memory perceives to be some negative aspect of those they deem "the other," or places "the others" or their culture in a less favorable light, then they would probably not consider that revisionist or politically correct history, but rather very good history and extremely well researched. It is only when the new account does the opposite of any of these that it earns the revisionist and politically correct label. Dan Kilgore and others have been verbally lynched by the anti-revisionists for claiming to have found evidence that Davy Crockett and a few others survived the Alamo battle and were executed after the battle. I suggest that if they had found evidence that Crockett had survived the battle and was able to talk and grin his way out of any further trouble and, after crossing his fingers and promising to never take up arms against the Mexican government again, he retired to Mississippi where, in 1846, he volunteered for the war with Mexico and, under an assumed name, fought throughout the war, killing thirty Mexican soldiers, and after the war he again retired to Mississippi where he established an orphanage for children whose parents had been killed by Indians and died on his 100th birthday when, during a bear hunting trip, he fell out of a tree, anti-revisionists would probably never claim that this was revisionist history, but on the contrary, excellent history. Why? Because it supported and reaffirmed what their collective memory has taught them about Crockett, Mexicans, and Indians.

There is one important difference between collective memory and folklore that should not be overlooked. Folklore comes from the people, the folk , while the power brokers of the dominant society often construct collective memory. As historian James Cobb has pointed out, "the most common foundation of group identity is a shared sense of a common past," and "the architects of group identities typically base their claims to distinctiveness and superiority on the vision of a glorious communal past." One of the most important sources of a group's or culture's knowledge of its communal past, in other words, its collective memory, is the history that is taught in its elementary and secondary schools. In years past, for many of us, that constituted the extent of our formal education in history. Our school boards, whether they are on the state or local level, determine what history is taught in our schools. Since, when I was in school, I failed to read any of these books and therefore have no idea what was taught at that time, I will have to refer you to what was taught in our schools in the 1930s. At that time, Texas school children were taught the following: "there is something about a cotton patch that seems to appeal to most Negroes. They look upon cotton picking as play, as a kind of game, rather than work. . . . But all people like to pick cotton after they are used to it."

Recently, revisionist and politically correct historians Thad Sinton and Dan Utley quoted an old cotton picker who told them, "You'd pick standing up until your back hurt so bad you could hardly stand it, and you'd get down on your knees and go along until your knees got to hurting so bad you couldn't stand it, and you'd get back up and bend over again. Something was always hurting." Those of you who have had the good fortune to have picked cotton know that the cotton picker Sinton and Utley talked to had it right and our school's textbook had it wrong on all accounts. The textbook contained one of Dobie's anecdotes of doubtful historicity that reveals more about a people than a book full of facts. The people, in this case, are the members of the school board. I believe it was Mark Twain who told us, "In the first place God made idiots. This was for practice. Then He made school boards."

What I have said is actually just a politically correct way to say that perhaps we have been lied to, and if so, a revision is long overdue and in order.

As we lawyers say, I rest and close.

The Evolution of Memory in a Small Texas Town: Janis Joplin and Port Arthur

Cynthia J. Beeman

I am getting a strong feeling of déjà vu standing up here. Many of you may remember I have done this before. Five years ago, when Dan Utley was president of the Association, emergency gall bladder surgery prevented him from delivering his presidential address, and I got to step in at the last minute and read his speech. I seriously considered returning the favor by drafting him to read this tonight, but then I decided giving up an organ to justify that idea was a bit extreme, so here I am.

The past several presidents have given insightful and interesting speeches about their personal stories and journeys as Texas historians. I considered following in that path and relating to you my own story, about my East Texas roots via my grandmother, Daisy, and her wacky sister, Lollie, from Gilmer. About how I, as a child, would scream at my dad from the back of the family station wagon to get him to stop so we could read historical markers along Texas highways. About how growing up with two older brothers and an older sister, I was inevitably influenced by their experiences, including an appreciation for the fascinating world of rock and roll music. About striking out for Austin after graduating from Texas Tech, convinced there would be some wonderful job for me there in the history field, and being fortunate enough to be hired at the Texas State Archives where I spent five years surrounded by primary source material. About discovering the Texas Women's History Project and volunteering with Ruthe Winegarten and her dedicated staff on that groundbreaking project. And about how I ended up at the Texas Historical Commission (THC), hired to write historical marker inscriptions, a job that I think made my dad as happy as it made me, remembering all those family vacations that took a bit longer than planned because he stopped the car to let me read markers along the way.

Instead, let me just tell you about two events that occurred early in my tenure as a THC staff historian, events that led to East Texas and, eventually, to the main topic of this speech. One day in June 1987, just a few months into my THC tenure, I took a phone call from a man at the Texas Milk Producers Association. It seems the group had, through a circuitous bankruptcy case, come into possession of a parcel of land in Nacogdoches County on which stood a two-story house bearing a historical marker. They wanted to sell the property, and luckily, someone on their staff realized the value of the historic structure and called the THC. It turns out the building was the old Half Way House, a stagecoach inn that originally stood in Chireno, halfway between San Augustine and Nacogdoches on the Camino Real. A previous owner had bought it, relocated it to his nearby farm, and then died, leaving it to begin a rapid deterioration due to neglect, storm damage, and exposure to the elements. Thus began my very first site visit as a THC historian. Our executive director, Curtis Tunnell, sent architectural historian Jim Steely and me to East Texas to get the full story and figure out what could be done to save the building. It is a rather long story, but suffice to say the house was saved, the folks in Chireno rallied together to get it back to its original community and restore it, and it is still one of my favorite historic preservation success stories. A major reason that trip stands out in my memory, though, is because that is when I first met Archie McDonald. He and Jere Jackson, who was then and is still the chair of the Nacogdoches County Historical Commission, spent a day driving with Jim and me along the back roads of the county to find the house, and their leadership and support helped form a coalition of folks that ultimately saved the building. Archie and I were friends from that day on, and after Gov. Ann Richards appointed him to the Texas Historical Commission, we worked together for many years and began a tradition involving jars of homemade fig preserves—but that's a story for another time.

The second event I'll tell you about from my first months at the THC involved another phone call, one that relates to the main topic of this talk, which, in a way, bookends my career as a THC historian. One of the structures in the THC office complex of historic buildings in Austin is the old Elrose Apartment building, and I quickly learned one of the urban legends about it was that Janis Joplin had lived there in the early 1960s during her brief time at the University of Texas. We have never been able to prove that claim, but right after I heard that story, I got a phone call from someone asking the THC to put up a marker for Janis Joplin in Port Arthur, her hometown. As a fan, I loved the idea. I immediately pictured the artwork on the album cover of "Cheap Thrills," her first record with Big Brother and the Holding Company, and remembered how I used to sneak into my brother's room and "borrow" his copy to listen to when he was not home. Unfortunately, though, according to the marker age rules in effect at the time, Janis didn't meet the program requirements, so I had to disappoint the caller and turn down the request.

Fast-forward twenty years, and one of the last marker applications approved before I retired from the THC was one for Janis Joplin, to be placed in front of her childhood home in Port Arthur. By that time I was the division director overseeing, among other things, the state marker program, so I invoked executive privilege and said I wanted to write the inscription for the Joplin marker. It was the last inscription I wrote and the last marker dedication I attended.

Reflecting on memories of growing up in a small Texas town in the 1950s and 1960s, I later decided to explore in more detail the story of how the passage of time and a shifting collective memory led to an evolution of Janis Joplin's legacy in her hometown. Most people in Port Arthur—many of them embarrassed by her drug use and public denigration of her hometown—wanted nothing to do with remembering her in the years following her death. But today she is celebrated with, among other things, a major museum exhibit and an Official Texas Historical Marker. I wanted to know how that transformation came about.

January 19, 2008, was a cold drizzly day in Port Arthur, Texas. A large crowd gathered that morning in a Baptist church fellowship hall on 32nd Street and sat reverently listening to Janis Joplin songs. The occasion was the dedication of an Official Texas Historical Marker on what would have been Joplin's sixty-fifth birthday. Few in attendance could picture her as a senior citizen. In their minds, she would forever be in her twenties—the queen of rock and roll, flamboyantly performing on stages around the world, her wild hair, colorful costumes, and feather boas flying as she belted out song after song in front of cheering audiences.

The event's celebratory mood represented a marked contrast from the town's attitude toward its most famous native daughter just a few decades earlier. Janis Joplin's relationship with her hometown was complicated. By most accounts, she enjoyed a normal, happy early childhood in a middle class family in the blue-collar refinery town, but her experiences as an outcast—some would say of her own making—in her high school years set the stage for rebellion and outrageous behavior that colored both her own memories and her legacy. As her fame in the 1960s hippie counterculture movement grew, she simultaneously wrote sentimental letters to her family, and made disparaging remarks about her hometown to reporters covering her meteoric rise in the music business. Lyrics written by her friend and fellow musician Kris Kristofferson could serve to sum up her journey: "(She's) a walkin' contradiction, partly truth and partly fiction, takin' every wrong direction on (her) lonely way back home."

Childhood friend Monteel Copple remembered riding bicycles around the tree-lined neighborhood streets with Janis and other playmates.

"We would always somehow meet up and ride around, and oftentimes go back to the schoolyard and play," she said. "We used to hang upside down on the monkey bars. We did not wear shorts—that was not heard of at the time—we all had dresses, and so we just would struggle to hold our dresses up to our knees while we were hanging upside down, and it would produce fits of insane giggles as we did that, you know, as only five- and six-year-olds can giggle. And that's what I remember so much about her, is the glee in her giggle. Just absolute unabandoned glee."

Janis' father built stilts, seesaws, tightropes, and other outdoor play equipment for his children and their friends who often gathered at the Joplin home. Janis and her sister and brother all did well in school and participated in various club and extracurricular activities. Janis sang in the elementary school glee club and joined a Bluebirds troop. During her junior high school years, she participated in community theater and volunteered at the local library.

But life began to change for Janis soon after she entered Thomas Jefferson High School in 1957. At first, she maintained a B grade average, and her high school yearbooks reveal she joined a number of clubs. At First Christian Church, "She sang in the adult choir because she had perfect pitch," remembered Yvonne Sutherlin, former chair of the Jefferson County Historical Commission. "She would sing any part at the last minute if someone didn't show up, or whatever the choir directors needed. She could sing it right that minute. She was very, very talented."

But soon Janis began to feel apart from those around her. Adolescent weight gain and a severe case of acne presaged a deep insecurity. In Port Arthur in the 1950s, physical appearance and adherence to social norms determined popularity and acceptance among high school students. As her standing among the school's in-crowd deteriorated, her response became one of defiance. According to one biographer, "Janis could have chosen to be inconspicuous, but she decided to fight what other girls accepted as fate." She embraced her outsider image in overt ways—dressing in tights and oversized men's shirts instead of the demure dresses or skirts worn by other girls, dying her hair orange, defying teachers who decried her behavior problems, and arguing with her parents. She read books by emerging Beat-era writers such as Jack Kerouac, Lawrence Ferlinghetti, and Allen Ginsberg, and openly questioned and challenged the conservative values of her family and community, particularly criticizing the town's racial segregation.

Joplin became friends with what her sister described as "a group of intellectuals"—boys she met in a community theater group who also questioned authority and the social status quo—and with them she began to push ever-widening boundaries. One of her friends said, "Everybody began to realize she was fun to have around because she raised so much hell. By the time we were in mid-high school, she was one of our favorite characters." She became what he described as a sort of court jester, whom they often used to shock their conservative classmates. "When Janis was outrageous, she was totally outrageous," he said. "We used it to our advantage when we wanted to freak people out."

Janis and her friends drove around town, built campfires at the beach, and gathered at an abandoned lighthouse to drink and talk. They climbed to the top of most of the water towers in the area, and clambered around on the girders underneath the top of the Rainbow Bridge that soared over the Neches River. Another of her friends recalled it as a symbolic action: "None of us planned on staying in Port Arthur," he said. "Whatever lay ahead, it was 'out there' somewhere. From a couple hundred feet above the Neches River . . . you could see there actually was a far horizon to reach toward."

But most significantly, Joplin and her friends listened to music, especially folk music, zydeco, and the blues and jazz that culturally migrated across the Sabine River from the juke joints and dives in Louisiana. As their late-night forays to bars on the other side of the river grew more frequent, they became enmeshed in the soulful music of artists such as Leadbelly, Big Mama Thornton, Bessie Smith, and Odetta, and soon Janis began singing in imitation of many of her musical inspirations. The more she sang, the more she seemed to find herself, although it was also at that time she began drinking to excess, a precursor of the addictive behavior that later defined her public persona.

Janis and her friends found trouble along with their musical excursions, and soon her reputation worsened and her relationship with her parents became more strained. She skated through her senior year in high school as a girl on the edges of acceptable behavior, on the outs with most of her classmates, but still finding creative expression through music and painting. She graduated with her class in the spring of 1960, and although some of her friends remembered it differently, after she became famous she told a number of interviewers her high school years were miserable because of cruel treatment by her classmates. In an oft-repeated quote, she told television talk show host Dick Cavett, "They laughed me out of class, out of town, and out of the state."

Following the path of many of her Port Arthur contemporaries, Joplin briefly attended Lamar State College of Technology in nearby Beaumont and Port Arthur College. In the spring of 1962, she left Port Arthur and enrolled at the University of Texas at Austin as an art student. She quickly fell in with a beatnik crowd at UT and spent most of her time at an off-campus apartment house on Nueces Street where many of them lived. Nicknamed the Ghetto, the ramshackle building was a haven for writers, artists, and musicians, and its freewheeling lifestyle suited Joplin's temperament. Captivated by folk music, she joined the musical group, the Waller Creek Boys, playing often at a café in the student union and at Threadgill's, the former gas station and beer joint on the old Dallas Highway run by country yodeler Kenneth Threadgill. Having found her calling, she became less of a student and more of a musician in Austin, and with that change came a headlong dive into the counterculture movement, complete with alcohol abuse, drug use, and sexual experimentation. By January 1963, she was only too willing to leave Texas behind and hitchhike to California to begin the next phase of her life.

Joplin's friends in San Francisco in the early 1960s included a number of fellow Austin émigrés, such as Jack Jackson, an innovative artist (and later award-winning historian) widely credited with creating the underground comics movement, and Chet Helms, band manager and later owner of the Avalon Ballroom music venue. With Helms' assistance, Joplin found jobs singing in coffeehouses and a few concert halls. But by the spring of 1965, she was dangerously underweight as a result of out-of-control drug use, and her worried friends put together a bus fare party to raise funds to send her home. She returned to Port Arthur intending to straighten out her life and reenroll in college, and she made an effort to do so for a while. But a year later, when Helms summoned her to the West Coast to become the "chick singer" for Big Brother and the Holding Company, she left home for the last time and made her way back to California.

Joplin's performances with Big Brother quickly drew widespread attention. Their appearance at the Monterey International Pop Festival, a three-day outdoor music event in June 1967, catapulted the band—and especially Joplin—to international fame. Reviews of the concert singled her out for praise and solidified her status as a rock and roll star. Big Brother and the Holding Company, with an increasing focus on lead singer Joplin, exploded onto the rock scene following the Monterey festival and with the release of its first album, *Cheap Thrills*.

As Joplin's star rose, her relationship with the members of the band deteriorated, and creative differences caused a parting of the ways by the end of 1968. She struck out on her own as a solo performer backed by a new group of musicians, which she christened Kozmic Blues. Hugely popular, and increasingly fueled by drugs and alcohol, she was a favorite topic of music journalists.

One writer, in a lengthy *New York Times* feature story, wrote about her reputation as a blues singer and as a hard-living rock star in early 1969. Saying "she consumes vast quantities of energy from some well inside herself that she believes is bottomless," he related her response to his questions concerning her lifestyle: "Yeah, I know I might be going too fast," she told him. "That's what a doctor said. He looked at me and said my liver is a little big, swollen, y'know. Got all melodramatic. I don't go back to him anymore. Man, I'd rather have 10 years of *super-hyper-most* than live to be 70 sitting in some chair . . . watching TV."

She also spoke about her hometown, and in one of the many harsh statements that later complicated her legacy in Port Arthur, she said, "I always wanted to be an artist. Port Arthur people thought I was a beatnik, and they didn't like beatniks, though they'd never seen one and neither had I. I read, I painted, I thought. There was nobody like me in Port Arthur. It was lonely, those feelings welling up and nobody to talk to. I was just 'silly crazy Janis.' Man, those people hurt me. It makes me happy to know I'm making it and they're back there, plumbers just like they were."

By 1970, Janis Joplin was arguably the most famous female rock and roll singer in the world. That summer, as she traveled the U.S. and Canada on concert tours and made plans to record a new album with her latest group of musicians, the Full Tilt Boogie Band, she also returned to Texas for two special events: a birthday concert honoring Kenneth Threadgill in Austin in June, and the tenth anniversary reunion of her high school class in Port Arthur in August.

Accompanied by an entourage of hippie friends sure to stand out in her hometown, Joplin arrived in Port Arthur on August 13, 1970, met by her parents and siblings, as well as the local press, at the airport. Her former classmates on the reunion committee, concerned the entire event would be overshadowed by her arrival, met with her the next morning and asked if she would agree to a press conference prior to the dinner and dance that evening, in part to stave off some of the harried press attention. She readily agreed, telling class president Sam Monroe she wanted to be treated like everybody else. As Monroe recalled later, "And of course she wasn't. I mean, she was a celebrity, and she was treated that way by her classmates."

One of Monroe's duties as emcee involved giving awards to people for various accomplishments, and in what was intended to be a humorous part of the program, he presented an automobile tire to Joplin for having traveled the farthest to attend the reunion. Janis, however, who by then was in a fragile emotional state—having burst on the scene earlier in the day with her trademark bravado, only to be left subdued by harsh questions from the hometown press—failed to appreciate the tongue-in-cheek effort at humor and felt disappointed to be given such a lowly token. What she hoped would be a triumphant homecoming, one in which she intended to flaunt her celebrity and importance to the town she felt had rejected her, instead turned bittersweet as, surrounded by her high school classmates, her old feelings of insecurity resurfaced.

Joplin returned to California, where plans for a new record with the Full Tilt Boogie Band began to take shape. By September they were recording in Los Angeles, with everyone involved pleased with and encouraged by the quality of the sessions. Despite the positive turn in her professional life, however, it soon became apparent to her dismayed friends that she was once again using heroin. On October 3, the band worked in the recording studio, laying down the instrumental track for a song on which Joplin would record vocals the following day. After the gathering broke up about eleven p.m., she briefly stopped at a bar on the way back to her room at the Landmark Hotel. At about one in the morning, apparently after injecting herself with a dose of heroin, she went to the lobby to get change to buy cigarettes. Returning to her room, she sat on the edge of the bed and almost immediately collapsed to the floor. When she failed to appear at the recording studio the following day, her road manager went to the hotel and discovered her body, the coins still clutched in her hand. The song she planned to record that day appeared on her final album, *Pearl*, in its unfinished, instrumental form. The title was "Buried Alive in the Blues."

News outlets around the world reported the death of the 27-year-old singer. Her hometown newspaper conveyed the news with the terse headline "Singer's Death Laid to Drugs" and said her parents had traveled to California to make funeral arrangements. The *Houston Post* said, "she lived like there was no tomorrow . . . and then suddenly there wasn't," and a *Time* magazine reporter wrote, she "died on the lowest and saddest of notes." The *Dallas Morning News* editorialized, "Janis Joplin did not have 10 years of 'superhypermost.' She literally exhausted herself to death, whether from drugs or simply from her pace of living, after only three years of stardom. But . . . she leaves behind her the work of a dedicated artist and the memory of a volatile but very human individual." According to Joplin's wishes, her friends and family spread her ashes along the coast of Northern California and later attended a wake to celebrate her life. She left funds for the party in her will and the invitation simply read, "The drinks are on Pearl."

For many years, although her fame grew elsewhere, Joplin's memory in Port Arthur reflected the negativity of her harsh words about her hometown and the disgrace associated with the manner of her death. Gradually, however, as appreciation of her musical legacy began to eclipse disapproval of her lifestyle, opinions started to change. By the mid-1980s, spurred on by her former classmates and friends, members of the local historical society and chamber of commerce began reassessing Joplin's legacy. Plans for an exhibit at Gates Memorial Library started to take shape. At Sam Monroe's request, Janis' mother provided letters, photographs, original artwork, scrapbooks, and numerous other artifacts for the exhibit. About the same time, John Palmer, a high school classmate, commissioned sculptor Doug Clark to create a multi-faced bronze bust of Joplin he intended to put on display in the Port Arthur Civic Center. City leaders rejected that idea, according to Monroe, so he suggested adding it to the library exhibit, with the official unveiling—ironically to be held at the civic center—set for January 19, 1988, Joplin's 45th birthday. According to Monroe, though, most local citizens remained opposed to recognizing Janis. A local radio station, on its Saturday morning call-in show, asked listeners to weigh in on whether the town should honor her. Monroe remembered everyone who called in said no. But at the same time, he was receiving calls from U.S. and international media outlets for radio, television, and newspaper interviews. He recalled, "I thought, my god, the city's going to get a black eye. We're going to unveil this bust to an audience of no local people, probably some national news people, and that'd be about it. So we broadened the concept to say we were going to honor all of Southeast Texas' legendary musicians, including Janis. Jerry LaCroix, "Count" Jackson of Boogie Kings fame, agreed to do a concert that night at the unveiling, so the whole thing worked."

Monroe continued the story, saying both Janis' brother Michael and her sister Laura came to the event. He was still concerned no one else would show up, but as they drove toward the civic center they saw lines of cars parked along the highway, and when they finally arrived at the parking lot, it was overflowing. "There were thousands of people everywhere!" he said. "Two television stations from Beaumont, two television stations from Houston, one from Lake Charles, one from Lafayette . . . they're all doing live broadcasts in the lobby of the Port Arthur Civic Center. And when the building over-filled—to what was estimated to be about five thousand people—the police cordoned off the building and refused to admit any additional people. And there were still about two thousand people outside. I never saw anything like that in my life. There hadn't been an event like that, in my experience, in this community, before or since. Just a phenomenon. There was just an outpouring of emotion. I get emotional thinking about it, because it was sort of a catharsis. People that night forgave Janis for all the negative [things] she'd said about the town and all. I think that was the turning point."

Port Arthur began not only to recognize Janis, but also to celebrate her legacy. The forgiveness and acceptance that Monroe believes began with the 1988 event grew into a form of civic boosterism as city leaders realized the potential for economic development based on her ties to the town. A focused program of heritage tourism promoting her fame and hometown connections brought thousands of visitors to the area. The city hosted an annual Janis Joplin Birthday Bash for a number of years, with guest concert artists such as the remaining members of Big Brother and the Holding Company and Kris Kristofferson. That event evolved into the Gulf Coast Music Hall of Fame and the Music Legends Exhibit Hall in the acclaimed Museum of the Gulf Coast, an institution that grew from the small display at Gates Memorial Library. Over the years, the Janis Joplin exhibit, anchored by a replica of her psychedelic-painted Porsche convertible, has remained a major attraction.

People still come from all around the world to pay homage to the queen of rock and roll who finally gained respect in her hometown. Billboards advertising the museum and Port Arthur appear along major highways in Texas, touting the area's history "from Jurassic to Joplin." A brochure offers a map and driving tour dubbed the Janis Joplin Road Trip that features sites associated with her life in Port Arthur, including the house where an Official Texas Historical Marker now honors the life of a small-town Texas girl who took every wrong direction on her lonely way back home.

Anti-Black Violence in Twentieth-Century East Texas

Bruce A. Glasrud

In August, 1919, John R. Shillady, the white executive secretary of the militant (to Texas whites, anyway) National Association for the Advancement of Colored People (NAACP) arrived in Austin to meet with Texas state political leaders about the state's harassment of NAACP locals, especially the one in Austin. He had a short, unproductive meeting with the interim attorney general, and received a subpoena to appear before a special court of inquiry, where he was verbally abused. The next day while walking, he was attacked and brutally beaten by a small mob of white men (bullies), some of whom were local politicians such as Dave Pickle. Nevertheless, Governor Hobby blamed Shillady for the attack and suggested that he and the NAACP leave the state. Shillady's resultant ill-mental and physical health forced him to resign.[1]

Why the white Texas suspicion of the NAACP? The answer is both simple and complicated. By the late summer of 1919, there were thirty-one local NAACP branches in the Lone Star state, with a membership of 7,046. Both the Dallas and San Antonio chapters held more than one thousand members each. This formidable black organization frightened white Texans bent on preserving "white supremacy." Shillady, too, as a white man from the north, was anathema to white Texans—he not only represented the "Yankee" north, he also espoused a belief in equality for black Texans. By late 1919, the NAACP had chastised white Texas behavior in reports on incidents in Waco, Houston, and Longview, among others. In fact, part of the rapid increase in NAACP membership in the state likely arose due to the eight-page special "Waco Horror" supplement published by the NAACP's *The Crisis* magazine.[2] Furthermore, the Shillady episode was representative of the overall white supremacist anti-black thoughts—blacks were inferior and must be kept in a subordinate place by any means necessary. To look further at these views and actions, this paper is going to focus on ten of the hundreds of twentieth-century Texas anti-black episodes.

Back to the larger question about white Texas' anti-black sentiments. Among the white beliefs were racism, fear of armed blacks, dislike of black male-white female relationships, and no or little education for blacks. White supremacy also served as a means to retain blacks in menial labor positions as well as to assure whites that they were indeed superior to blacks. Neil Foley's *The White Scourge* and William Carrigan's *The Making of a Lynching Culture* also emphasize the changes transpiring in modern, twentieth century Texas—changes that frightened white Texans, such as an increase in black resistance. As Carrigan noted, the other changes included "changing immigration patterns, demographic shifts, technological changes, formalization of disfranchisement, implementation of rigid residential segregation, and the rise of a new consumer culture."³ Lynching and mob violence, including riots and pogroms, were the principal means of enforcing white supremacy. In addition to Foley and Carrigan, there are a number of other informative studies on this issue; they include three master's theses, two articles, and one other book, Jacqueline Dowd Hall's *Revolt Against Chivalry*.⁴

Even though nearly five hundred lynchings took place in Texas prior to 1930, and one hundred African Texans solely were lynched in the first decade of the twentieth century, it was the troubling 1916 lynching at Waco that brought specific attention to Texas and led to the growth of the NAACP. The incident became known as "The Waco Horror" due to its heinous nature. Jesse Washington, an illiterate black teenager, was accused and found guilty of murder and rape of a white woman. Although no evidence or proof existed (he was forced to plead guilty), he was taken from the courthouse by a crazed, white mob, dragged through town, his extremities cut off, chained to a tree, hung, and burned. After all that, and while photos were taken, his body was dragged through town, with parts sold for souvenirs. In spite of the photos, no one was arrested or tried for this horrendous murder. Even *The Crisis*' dramatic and important supplement had produced photos to no avail.⁵ This cruel incident has been mentioned by many scholars and authors; the most thorough explanation and study is Patricia Bernstein's, *The First Waco Horror: The Lynching of Jesse Washington and the Rise of the NAACP*. Two other works should be mentioned: Rogers Melton Smith's "The Waco Lynching of 1916: Perspective and Analysis" and James M. SoRelle's "The 'Waco Horror': The Lynching of Jesse Washington."⁶

The white Texas fear of armed blacks can be noted in a variety of ways, but especially in the distrust of black soldiers of the United States Army. Various incidents in the early twentieth century at El Paso, Del Rio, Waco, and especially Brownsville have been written about and discussed well by Garna Christian and also James Leiker.⁷ But it was the 1917 "Houston Riot or Mutiny" that depicted the attitudes most distinctly.

On August 23, 1917, some recently stationed, mistreated black soldiers of the Twenty-fourth Infantry fought with white police and citizens of Houston. Twenty people were killed.

Even though Secretary of War Newton D. Baker told Pres. Woodrow Wilson that the basic causes of the trouble were "the so-called Jim Crow laws" of Houston, that view did not prevail in Houston or even in the military. Ultimately, 110 black soldiers were sentenced to death or life imprisonment by military courts-martial, even though each claimed innocence. Thirteen were secretly killed, even before any other military or civilian review could be accomplished. Scholars who studied the episode in general agreed that black soldiers were involved, but two other approaches follow. Robert V. Haynes, in *A Night of Violence: The Houston Riot of 1917*, puts blame on the soldiers, as did the courts-martial. However, Calvin Smith, in two well-constructed articles, argues persuasively that it was the white citizens of Houston who were to blame. From the first entrance of the black soldiers in Houston, the citizens, and especially the police, had vigorously enforced Jim Crow laws and disdainfully treated the black soldiers not as men of the U.S. Army, but as interlopers. Smith's general interpretation agreed with that of Secretary of War Newton Baker.[8] Other studies of the riot or mutiny included, as usual, an NAACP investigation, two master's theses, two articles, and a refreshing analysis by Arthur E. Barbeau and Florette Henri in their broader history, *The Unknown Soldiers: African American Troops in World War I*.[9]

By the summer of 1919, the First World War was over and black as well as white soldiers returned to their homes in the Lone Star state. Black soldiers, back from "making the world safe for democracy," determined that they too would benefit from democracy. On June 17, in Longview, the sheriff turned over to a local mob a black man accused of being in love with a white woman, who likely returned the feeling. The black man was lynched. Soon an article appeared in the *Chicago Defender* describing the incident. A black teacher, accused of writing the article, was severely beaten by a group of whites, and when even more—a mob—arrived at his house to attack the man, the white mob was greeted by armed resistance from friends and supporters of the black man. Whites set fire to two homes, including that of the teacher as well as a dance hall. Texas Rangers and the state National Guardsmen went to Longview to prevent further violence; they arrested seventeen whites and twenty-one blacks, but no one went to court.[10]

Blacks sent notice at Longview that they would and could defend themselves. Among the friends of the teacher was the black medical doctor in Longview. The riot is well-documented, including W. E. B. Du Bois's *Crisis* article. Later efforts of particular help are articles by Kenneth Durham, George Ohler, William Tuttle, and Jared Wheeler. Annette Moye included Longview in her master's thesis, "Major Race

Riots in the Red Summer of 1919;" Arthur Waskow and Harry Krenek both mentioned the Longview Riot in chapters in their books. Lawrence Olson's Southwest Texas State University thesis, "Black Texans in the Red Summer of 1919," covered the topic well.[11] A relative of the doctor, Sarah Davis Elias, added to our understanding with two works, one a master's thesis at Morgan State University and the other an interesting book, *Recalling Longview: An Account of the Longview, Texas Riot, July 11, 1919*. Any future investigation cannot overlook her studies.[12]

As noticed in the aforementioned confrontations, Texas' urban centers, such as Austin, Waco, Houston, and Longview, frequently occupy center stage when one discusses racial atrocities in the Lone Star state. However, the largest number of such anti-black incidents took place in rural East Texas. In 1910, for example, whites in Anderson County ran around killing blacks apparently without any cause or provocation. The episode since has been referred to as the "Slocum Massacre." Ultimately, in this racial pogrom, eighteen black Texas citizens were killed.[13] Twelve years later in rural Freestone County another violent anti-black episode took place as revealed by Monte Akers in *Flames After Midnight: Murder, Vengeance, and the Desolation of a Texas Community*. In the small, thriving community of Kirven, a young white woman was brutally murdered. Even though evidence pointed the way toward the killer or killers (who were white), whites determined blacks guilty. Three innocent black men were burned alive (they were tied to a plow to keep them upright and alive longer), three others also soon lynched, and a month long reign of terror ensued. Once more, blacks were killed with impunity; the number of black deaths ranged from eleven to twenty-three. Eventually Kirven and Freestone County whites arrived at Simsboro and killed two more African American citizens. Other Simsboro blacks armed themselves, joined together, and convinced the white marauders that neither side wanted to die. The Kirven-Simsboro episode ended. No whites received convictions and the real murderers went free. Blacks immediately left Kirven, whites soon after, and the town virtually disappeared. Nationally, anti-lynching discussions increased as did editorials from Texas newspapers. The actual specifics were not determined until Akers' thorough and convincing research.[14] A few of us mentioned the incident in earlier studies, but that is all. Carrigan clearly summarized the incident: "in Freestone County on the edge of central Texas, a brutal act of racial violence occurred in May 1922. A mob in Kirven burned three black men alive, then went on a month long binge of racial intimidation and terrorism. Meanwhile local authorities concealed the identity of the probable white murderers."[15]

By 1930, economic problems fostered by the onset of the depression led to tensions between black and white tenant farmers; the city of Sherman also experienced monetary difficulties that fed anti-black attitudes. The Sherman Riot of 1930 stemmed from the arrest of a black man who allegedly assaulted a white woman; officials called the Texas Rangers to protect the prisoner, and they did so for a time. After placing the black man in a vault for his protection, though, a mob set fire to the courthouse and burned the victim alive. Next, the mob acquired the black man's body, hooked it to a car, and dragged it through the streets. They then tied it up and burned it. The rangers left and the rioters immediately looted and burned the black section of town, and virtually seized control of Sherman. When troops of the Texas National Guard arrived, the mob attacked them, and before martial law restored order, more homes and businesses in the African American section of town were destroyed. Prominent western historian Robert M. Utley referred to the Sherman fiasco as "one of the most brutish and shameful episodes in the history of Texas."[16] The black section of town, alive with thriving businesses prior to the riot, never recovered, and numerous black leaders and workers left the area. Many historians have explored he riot in 1930 Sherman. Mike Cox and Robert Utley related it to Texas Ranger history and Harry Krenek to that of the Texas National Guard. The best single article on the riot is that of Edward Hake Phillips, originally published in the *East Texas Historical Journal*. Other writers included Durward Pruden, whose sociological thesis did not mention names or the city, Arthur Franklin Raper, whose 1934 book is a classic, and Nolan Thompson. For a fictionalized account by a prominent black author, see Njoki McElroy, "The Ninth Day of May."[17]

Changes precipitated by World War II set off a violent race riot in 1943 Beaumont. Employment in the shipyards opened to blacks and as a result competitive tensions between white and black workers increased. Early in June a black man allegedly raped a white Beaumont telephone operator; police eventually shot and killed the man as he likely resisted arrest. Ten days later violence flared when on June 15 and 16, whites and blacks clashed after white Beaumont shipyard workers learned that a white woman had accused a black man of raping her. On the evening of June 15 more than two thousand angry and alarmed workers started walking downtown. As they were moving toward city hall, the size of the mob grew, and ultimately the crowd reached four thousand. Even though the woman could not identify the suspect (a few reports indicate she fabricated the event), the white workers and other mob partisans began breaking into stores in the black section of downtown Beaumont proceeded to terrorize black neighborhoods in the central and north sections of the city. Many blacks were assaulted, several restaurants and stores were pillaged, a number of buildings were burned, and more than one hundred African American homes were ransacked. Eventually, more than two hundred people were arrested, fifty were injured, and two were killed. The Texas State Guard and Texas Rangers were called in to halt the devastation, though too late for the black structures. No one was convicted. With martial law established, one interesting twist emerged: black workers were not allowed to go to work, but white workers were allowed to work. The Beaumont Race Riot could stand some new study; however, two first rate articles covering this affair have been published, one by James A. Burran and one by James S. Olson and Sharon Phair.[18]

As has been noted, race violence, that is, anti-black race violence, was a consistent and overwhelming threat to black Texans during the first half of the twentieth century. It continued, although with occurrences. As many know, race violence took place during the civil rights era in the Lone star state, even though pressures existed to both overlook the violence and to try to prevent its occurrence. But violence broke out in Mansfield High School, the Texas governor and attorney general raided the offices of the NAACP, and in 1967, a riot took place at Texas Southern University. The blame for the latter depended on who you asked; the police blamed black youths and the black community blamed the police. An article needs to be written on this episode. Other violent occasions also presented themselves. However, for this paper I am going to jump all the way from 1943 to lesser known incidents that transpired in 1980 and afterward.

Early in the twentieth century, as I have noted, white suspicions that a black man assaulted a white woman often led to a lynching and occasionally to a riot. Some conditions change, whether due to public pressure, new laws, or more robust police and legal scrutiny. In August 1980, in Conroe, the nude body of a dead young white female student was discovered. Soon a black man, Clarence Brandley, the school janitor, was arrested (with no reason or evidence except that he was a black man) for the murder. This whole episode has been written about in a book by Nick Davies entitled *White Lies*. White lies from the district attorney, a Texas Ranger, other local officials, and in a way the white people of Conroe led to his conviction by an all-white jury. A legal lynching, as opposed to the early twentieth century version, was in progress. However, after nine years of incarceration and life on death row, Clarence Brandley won his freedom. He never returned to Conroe, probably wisely.[19]

In eight months of 1987 and 1988, black Texans Troy Lee Starling,

Loyal Garner, Jr., and Kenneth "Hambone" Simpson died within one hundred miles of each other in a triangular part of the East Texas pine thickets. Each met death at the hands of white lawmen; the last faces they saw were white law officers. Starling was shot through the back of the neck by a .357 magnum issued by the Texas DPS. Simpson's body was tied down in a small jail cell; eleven officers had been in the room with him. His body was horribly beaten. Only the death of Garner, severely beaten with a blackjack, faced a challenge in the court system. Garner's beating was not isolated; during the course of the ensuing trials. considerable evidence indicated that in Hemphill beatings in the jail were common. We know about this case due to the energy and ability of a tireless writer, Texas native Howard Swindle, whose book, *Deliberate Indifference: A Story of Racial Injustice and Murder*, compellingly takes us through this episode of Texas racial violence. There is also a song about the case, "The Ballad of Loyal Garner, Jr."[20]

Eleven years after the Loyal Garner murder, in one other small town in East Texas, Jasper, a forty-nine year old black man, James Byrd, Jr., walked home from a party. Three white men in a pickup truck offered Byrd a ride home, and he willingly accepted. Soon the men drove away from Byrd's home to a wooded patch. At some point, Byrd was tortured, chained to the back of the pickup, and dragged to his death. Portions of his body lay in various parts of the road. His unchained body was dropped off near a church. This crime of hate received national attention. Ultimately, the three men were convicted, two of them receiving death sentences. Two of the men served time in prison together and joined white supremacist groups. One had a tattoo of a black man hanging. Three authors have written books about the episode, but in a disheartening note for academics and historians, none includes a bibliography. However, each is good; as the titles suggest, the three authors developed their stories from differing perspectives: Joyce King's *Hate Crime: The Story of a Dragging in Jasper, Texas*, Dina Temple-Raston's *Death in Texas: A Story of Race, Murder, and a Small Town's Struggle for Redemption*, and Ricardo C. Ainslie, *Long Dark Road: Bill King and Murder in Jasper, Texas*.[20]

Unfortunately, we in the "modern" twenty-first century cannot yet escape the hatred that brings about racism in our midst—this in spite of the fact that we even have an African American President of the United States. Two twenty-first century East Texas incidents bear mention. The first concerns a mentally disabled, forty-plus year old African American, Billy Ray Johnson, who in 2003, at Linden, was beaten severely at a party to which he had been driven. There he had been teased relentlessly by four white males prior to being beaten. His body was later dumped by the side of the road. Ultimately, each of the white men was judged not guilty by juries in Linden. In fact, the people of Linden blamed the victim, not the four "good" white youths. Johnson survived; later, in a civil trial sponsored by the Southern Poverty Law Center (SPLC), he received a nine million dollar settlement from a Cass County jury. He could at least be taken out of a rest home. For information on this case, read the *Texas Monthly* article, "The Beating of Billy Ray Johnson," by Pamela Colloff. It was so good the SPLC received permission to reprint it and distributed the article to its membership.[22]

Five years later, in September 2008, a black man, Brandon McClelland, nicknamed "Big Boy" for his substantial size, rode with two white fellow workers to locate some beer. When he got out of the pickup, he was first hit and run over, then dragged between forty and seventy feet underneath the carriage of the truck. This incident took place in Paris, which for over a century featured other dastardly examples of anti-black brutality. The police took a long time to determine what happened—blacks say too long. At least one report refers to the Paris murder as a "Jasper-style lynching."[23]

In the year 2013, it is difficult to believe that anti-black behavior on the part of some whites, still exists. Yet, we can only look to Florida and the Trayvon Martin case and to the long brutal history of anti-black race violence in East Texas. Conditions for blacks have improved. We do not have a yearly listing of lynchings anymore, and even separate incidents are more likely to have a few years in between before the next one takes place. Yet, they still occur.

In this report, I have emphasized a few of the vicious anti-black patterns of behavior that transpired in twentieth-century East Texas. Such episodes come about due to intense dislike of African Americans by the white aggressors. Perhaps this type of feeling is spurred by a more general belief on the part of too many white Texans that not only can and should blacks be kept in their place, but they also should not be able to vote, to hold office, or to have a responsible job. In others, the anti-black behavior is fomented by politicians, by law officers, and by the general public, who believe that "good" old boys could not have brutally killed a black man, even with the evidence directly in front of them. We can only hope for a better future.

NOTES

1. NAACP, *Mobbing of John R. Shillady, Secretary of the National Association for the Advancement of Colored People* (New York: NAACP, October 1919), 1-11.

2. Ibid.

3. Neil Foley, *The White Scourge: Mexicans, Blacks, and Poor Whites in Texas Cotton Culture* (Berkeley: University of California Press, 1997); William D. Carrigan, *The Making of a Lynching Culture: Violence and Vigilantism in Central Texas, 1836-1916* (Urbana: University of Illinois Press, 2004), quote on page 184.

4. David L. Chapman, "Lynching in Texas" (Master's thesis, Texas Tech University, 1973); Mary Elizabeth Estes, "An Historical Survey of Lynchings in Oklahoma and Texas" (Master's thesis, University of Oklahoma, 1942); Bruce A. Glasrud, "Child or Beast? White Texas' View of Blacks, 1900-1910," *East Texas Historical Journal* 15.2 (1977), 38-44; Jacquelyn Dowd Hall, *Revolt Against Chivalry: Jessie Daniel Ames and the Women's Campaign Against Lynching* (New York: Columbia University Press, 1979); Brandon Jett, "Paris is Burning: Lynching and Racial Violence in Lamar County, 1890-1920," *East Texas Historical Journal* 51.2 (2013), 40-64; David W. Livingston, "The Lynching of Negroes in Texas, 1900-1925" (Master's thesis, East Texas State University, 1972).

5. NAACP, *Mobbing of John R. Shillady, Secretary of the National Association for the Advancement of Colored People* (New York: NAACP, October 1919), 1-11.

6. Patricia Bernstein, *The First Waco Horror: The Lynching of Jesse Washington and the Rise of the NAACP* (College Station: Texas A&M University Press, 2005); Rogers Melton Smith, "The Waco Lynching of 1916: Perspective and Analysis" (Master's thesis, Baylor University, 1971); James M. SoRelle, "The 'Waco Horror': The Lynching of Jesse Washington," *Southwestern Historical Quarterly* 86.4 (April 1983), 517-37; James M. SoRelle, "Jesse Washington Lynching," *The Handbook of Texas Online* (http://www.tshaonline.org/handbook).

7. Garna Christian, *Black Soldiers in Jim Crow Texas, 1899-1917* (College Station: Texas A&M University Press, 1993); James N. Leiker, *Racial Borders: Black Soldiers along the Rio Grande* (College Station: Texas A&M University Press, 2002).

8. Robert V. Haynes, *A Night of Violence: The Houston Riot of 1917* (Baton Rouge: Louisiana State University Press, 1976); Robert V. Haynes, "The Houston Mutiny and Riot of 1917," *Southwestern Historical Quarterly* 76 (1973), 418-39; C. Calvin Smith, "The Houston Riot of 1917, Revisited," *Houston Review* 13 (1991), 84-102; C. Calvin Smith, "On the Edge: The Houston Riot of 1917," *The Griot* 10 (Spring 1991), 3-12.

9. Thomas Richard Adams, "The Houston Riot of 1917" (Master's thesis, Texas A& M University, 1972); Arthur E. Barbeau and Florette Henri, *The Unknown Soldiers: African-American Troops in World War I* (1974; New York: Da Capo Press, 1996), 26-32, 210-211; Martha Gruening, "Houston: An NAACP Investigation," *The Crisis* 15 (November 1917), 14-19; Phocion Samuel Park, Jr., "The Twenty-Fourth Infantry Regiment and the Houston Riot of 1917" (Master's thesis, University of Houston, 1971); Edgar A. Schuler, "The Houston Race Riot, 1917," *Journal of Negro History* 29 (July 1944), 300-338; C. D. Waide, "When Psychology Failed: An Unbiased Fact-Story of the Houston Race Riot of 1917," *Houston Gargoyle*, May 15, 22, 29, 1928; June 5, 12, 1928.

10. Kenneth R. Durham, "The Longview Race Riot of 1919," *East Texas Historical Journal* 18 (1980), 13-24; Kenneth R. Durham, 'The Longview Riot of 1919," *The Handbook of Texas Online* (http://www.tshaonline.org/handbook); William N. Tuttle, Jr., "Violence in a Heathen Land: The Longview Race Riot of 1919," *Phylon* 33 (Winter 1972), 324-333.

11. W. E. B. DuBois, "The Riot at Longview, Texas," *Crisis* 18 (October 1919), 296-298; Harry Krenek, "Race Riots at Longview and Sherman," in *The Power Vested: The Use of Martial Law and the National Guard in Texas Domestic Crisis, 1919-1932* (Austin: Presidial Press, 1980), 105-137; Annette Moye, "'Longview,'" in "Major Race Riots in the Red Summer of 1919" (Master's thesis, Texas Southern University, 1971), 22-27; George Ohler, "Background Causes of the Longview Race Riot of July 10, 1919," *Journal of the American Studies Association of Texas* 12 (1981), 46-54; Lawrence Olsen, "Black Texans in the 'Red Summer' of 1919: The Longview Race Riot" (Master's thesis, Southwest Texas State University, 1974); William N. Tuttle, Jr., "Violence in a Heathen Land: The Longview Race Riot of 1919," *Phylon* 33 (Winter 1972), 324-333; Arthur I. Waskow, *From Race Riot to Sit-in, 1919 and the 1960s* (Garden City, New York: Doubleday, 1966), 16-20; Jared Wheeler, "Prelude to Anarchy: The Longview Race Riot of 1919," *The Texas Ranger Dispatch* 30 (Fall 2009), 4-14.

12. Sarah Davis Elias, "Grimshaw's Ecological Analysis of the Longview Riot" (Master's thesis, Morgan State University, 1974); Sarah Davis Elias, *Recalling Longview: An Account of the Longview, Texas Riot, July 11, 1919* (Baltimore: C. H. Fairfax Company, 2004).

13. Bruce A. Glasrud, "Black Texans, 1900-1930: A History" (Ph.D. dissertation, Texas Tech University, 1969), 149-150; *Fort Worth Star-Telegram*, July 30, 31, 1910.

14. Monte Akers, *Flames after Midnight: Murder, Vengeance, and the Desolation of a Texas Community* (Austin: University of Texas Press, 1999).

15. Carrigan, *Making of a Lynching Culture*, 192; Glasrud, "Black Texans,"166-167.

16. Edward Hake Phillips, "The Sherman Courthouse Riot of 1930," *East Texas Historical Journal* 25.2 (1987), 12-19; Robert M. Utley, *Lone Star Lawmen* (New York: Penguin, 2007), 133-140, quote on p. 134.

17. Mike Cox, "The Sherman Riot," in *Texas Ranger Tales II* (Plano, Tex.: Republic of Texas Press, 1999), 193-205; Harry Krenek, "Race Riots at Longview and Sherman," in *The Power Vested: The Use of Martial Law and the National Guard in Texas Domestic Crisis, 1919-1932* (Austin: Presidial Press, 1980), 105-137; Durward Pruden, "A Sociological Study of a Texas Lynching" (Master's thesis, Southern Methodist University, 1935); Arthur Franklin Raper, "Burning Down the Courthouse: Sherman, Grayson County, Texas," *The Tragedy of Lynching* (Chapel Hill: University of North Carolina Press, 1933), 319-355; Nolan Thompson, "Sherman Riot of 1930," *The Handbook of Texas Online* (http://www.tshaonline.org/handbook); Njoki McElroy, "The Ninth Day of May," in Suzanne Comer, *Common Bonds: Stories By and About Modern Texas Women* (Dallas: Southern Methodist University Press, 1990): 40-42.

18. James A. Burran, "Violence in an 'Arsenal of Democracy': The Beaumont Race Riot, 1943," *East Texas Historical Journal* 14.1 (1976), 39-51; James S. Olson and Sharon Phair, "The Anatomy of a Race Riot: Beaumont, Texas, 1943," *Texana* 11 (1973), 64-72. See also James S. Olson, "Beaumont Riot of 1943," *Handbook of Texas Online* (http://tshaonline.org/handbook) and Tabitha C. Wang, "Beaumont Race Riot, 1943," *Blackpast Online Encyclopedia* (http://www.blackpast.org).

19. Nick Davies, *White Lies: Rape, Murder, and Justice Texas Style* (New York: Avon Books, 1991).

20. Howard Swindle, *Deliberate Indifference: A Story of Racial Injustice and Murder* (New York: Viking Penguin, 1993).

21. Ricardo C. Ainslie, *Long Dark Road: Bill King and Murder in Jasper, Texas* (Austin: University of Texas Press, 2004); Joyce King, *Hate Crime: The Story of a Dragging in Jasper, Texas* (New York: Random House, 2002); Dina Temple-Raston, *Death in Texas: A Story of Race, Murder, and a Small Town's Struggle for Redemption* (New York: Henry Holt, 2002).

22. Pamela Colloff, "The Beating of Billy Ray Johnson," *Texas Monthly* (February 2007); also a special insert reprinted and distributed by the Southern Poverty Law Center.

23. Gretel C. Kovach and Arian Campo-Flores, "Problems in Paris, Texas," *Newsweek* (February 9, 2009), 44-45; Jesse Muhammad, "Jasper-style Lynching in Paris, Texas?" (http://finalcall.com/artman/publish/printer_5348.shtml). On earlier Paris anti-black behavior, see Brandon Jett, "Paris is Burning: Lynching and Racial Violence in Lamar County, 1890-1920," *East Texas Historical Journal* 51.2 (2013), 40-64.

East Texas and the Battle for Texas' Past

Gene B. Preuss

Political cartoonist Jules Feiffer published an illustration in 1970 of a man wearing a hard hat who states, "When I went to school I learned George Washington never told a lie, slaves were happy on the plantation, the men who opened the West were giants, and we won every war because God was on our side." The cartoon man continues, "But where my kid goes to school he learns George Washington was a slave owner, slaves hated slavery, the men who opened the West committed genocide, and the wars we won were victories for U.S. imperialism." Confounded, the man rationalizes, "No wonder my kid's not an American. They're teaching him some other country's history." The increased marriage of the social sciences and history in the mid-twentieth century was changing the narrative of the American past.

The cartoon illustrates the importance of how and when we teach history; for history is the narrative of our past, it is how we identify ourselves, and in some sense tells us about what our state and our nation are, and who we—as Texans and Americans—are, or want ourselves to be, and be seen. In 1968, cognitive psychologist David Ausubel stated, "the most important single factor influencing learning is what the learner already knows."[1] In Texas schools, students take world civilizations and history courses in the fourth, seventh, eighth, and eleventh grades. Given the numerous touch points at which students are exposed to history classes, it is little wonder that American and, in the Lone Star State, Texas history, has been such a political issue.

In September 2014, the news media drew attention to a story that members of the Texas State Board of Education (SBOE) wanted to require the College Board's Advanced Placement History exam to conform to the 2010 history standards for Texas. SBOE members were concerned that the AP history exams were trying to sneak in aspects of the Common Core, a national curriculum rejected by Texas. The State Board allowed the Advanced Placement (AP) and International Baccalaureate (IB) curriculums into Texas public schools as acceptable alternatives to the Board of Education's approved public school curriculum, the Texas Essential Knowledge and Skills (TEKS). News that the College Board's new revised exam placed less emphasis on memorizing names and dates, and instead required critical thinking and interpretive skills provoked conservative ire. The *Houston Chronicle* reported that a conservative activist complained, "This new APUSH (Advanced Placement U.S. History), the professional development of the teachers, is using the Common Core progressive teaching strategies, versus the old APUSH allowed for the Texas TEKS to be taught in the classroom." It was another concern about the deterioration of "traditional" American history.[2]

Two years earlier, Texas Republicans drew criticism from many news reporters, media pundits, and talk show comedians when their 2012 party platform seemed to oppose "critical thinking" for schoolchildren. The plank in the party platform stated, "We oppose the teaching of Higher Order Thinking Skills (HOTS) (values clarification), critical thinking skills and similar programs that are simply a relabeling of Outcome-Based Education (OBE) (mastery learning) which focus on behavior modification and have the purpose of challenging the student's fixed beliefs and undermining parental authority."[3] Some opined that whomever drafted the platform plank conflated "critical thinking" with such demonized pedagogical terms like "outcomes based education." Although Texas Republican Party spokesperson Chris Elam stated the inclusion of "critical thinking skills" was an "oversight," but not before it created a social media firestorm.[4]

In 2010, the national, and even international, media focused a spotlight on the Lone Star State as the State Board of Education began reviewing the history components for the Texas Essential Knowledge and Skills, the state-approved public school curriculum. Although the process started out quietly enough, by the end of 2009 and early in 2010, public comments and criticism had drawn attention from conservatives and liberals alike over the ideological bent of the proposed history textbook standards. Headlines and political pundits drew the media's interest when they said Thomas Jefferson was going to be removed from books. Others claimed that the "radical members of the education establishment" and "liberal activists hijacked Texas' social studies curriculum process" and were working to remove the Christian family values upon which our Founding Fathers built the Constitution.[5]

In 1998, the Lubbock Independent School District adopted art books for its curriculum despite protests from some citizens who believed Rembrandt's painting, "The Return of the Prodigal Son," representing a young man kneeling in front of an older man with three others looking on, might be too risqué for young audiences. The Lubbock school superintendent, Curtis Culwell, acknowledged "when he thinks of Rembrandt he thinks of one of the Teenage Mutant Ninja Turtles" (although none of the turtles is named Rembrandt"). Culwell defended the educational benefits of the books. "I have a good friend who told me once, 'I don't know art, but I know naked,' and there's none of that in these books," Culwell insisted.[6]

What the public saw was a series of battles in the Culture Wars that had attracted media attention since the 1990s. In their book, *History on Trial: Culture Wars and the Teaching of the Past*, Gary Nash, Charlotte Crabtree, and Ross Dunn observed that "the 'culture war' that broke out suddenly in the fall of 1994 when Lynn Cheney, Dick Cheney's wife and the former chair of the National Endowment for the Humanities, criticized the National Standards for History in a *Wall Street Journal* editorial ominously titled, "The End of History."[7]

In the editorial, Cheney predicted a gloomy future American history education. She claimed a confidential source informed her that Clinton's election "unleashed the forces of political correctness" among professional historians that would lead to the decline of "traditional history" in favor of "the revisionist agenda" of African-American and other minority historians and "their great hatred for traditional history." The result, she warned, would be "that much that is significant in our past will begin to disappear from our schools."[8]

But, fears of a decline in American historical knowledge originated much earlier than the 1990s. Four decades earlier, historian Richard Hofstadter wrote that what he termed "Anti-Intellectualism" in American cultural history had indeed been a longstanding tradition in American thought. In 1943, newspapers reported that a survey of college students in the United States demonstrated that many did not know some basic facts about American history.[9] They could not identify the original thirteen colonies or identify prominent businessmen, and they did not know that Thomas Jefferson had been a US president or the author of a majority of the Declaration of Independence. While Lynn Cheney may have ignited the most recent history culture war, the battles over how history is taught in the public schools dates back before World War II.

In 1932, prior to the upcoming Texas Centennial, the Texas Legislature decreed the first week of March would be "Texas Week," but the lawmakers cautioned, "under no condition, is Texas Week to be looked upon as a week of holidays; but on the other hand and quite to the contrary, it is hereby alleged that during Texas Week every citizen of this State is encouraged to work, insofar as he is able, and to do his work a bit better than he does it during other weeks of the year."[10]

The proclamation encouraged "every home; every office, place of business and industry; every school, parochial, private, or public; every college and university; and all institutions of whatever class or character" and prescribed a list of suggestions for celebrating Texas Week in a pervasive effort to get that "every citizen, old or young, within the borders of this great State be urged now and ever in the future . . . to exalt and extol the cultural and spiritual values which we cherish so fondly; the blessed and romantic traditions of our glorious history; the high standards and lofty ideals of statesmanship, of scholarship, of leadership, of character and of service which our forefathers gave to us as our rare and rich heritage, and to give thanks for this marvelous inheritance as we faithfully and conscientiously observe Texas Week." Clearly, the legislators wanted Texans to embrace in a patriotic way the "romantic traditions" of the state's heritage. This also would pave the way for the upcoming Texas Centennial in 1936.

There was also a concerted effort to inculcate into American schoolchildren an appreciation for US and state history during the depression, when many believed that desperate people might be swayed by radical political philosophies, and other "isms" like communism or fascism, that were gaining popularity in Europe. Conservatives also worried that New Deal programs were really "creeping socialism." Following World War II, the increasing power of the Soviet Union and the communist takeover of China, and aggression in Korea led many Americans to fear that democracy was threatened internationally. Even US attempts to "contain" international communism with the US signing of NATO (North Atlantic Treaty Organization) and other similar treaties,came under criticism for subverting American interests. In the 1950s, Wisconsin senator Joseph McCarthy played on these fears and announced his determination to weed out communists and "fellow travelers" in the highest positions of US government. Conservative organizations like the John Birch Society also warned of communist and totalitarian subversion.

Many Texans were likewise anticommunist, and joined the John Birch Society and welcomed the McCarthy crusade. Some had previously supported the work of East Texas Congressman Martin Dies, who helped launch the US House's committee that became the House Un-American Activities committees.[11] In 1951, the Texas Communist Control Law required all state employees, including schoolteachers and other school employees, to take an oath they were "not, and have never been a member of the Communist Party, " or other subversive organization included on a list drawn up by the US Attorney General and the Texas Department of Public Safety.[12]

In 1947, the Supreme Court ruled in *Everson v. Board of Education* that the First Amendment constituted a "wall of separation between church and state." Outraged lawmakers included the phrase "under God" in the Pledge of Allegiance, and ordered the phrase, "In God We Trust" to be printed on all US currency.[13] Religion became as important to the notion of Americanism as patriotism and state and national heritage. A *Houston Chronicle* reader conveyed what many already believed: "The overwhelming majority of the American people all along was always in favor of religion having the right of way."[14] West Texas conservative rancher and historian J. Evetts Haley was behind a movement to get the legislature to mandate six hours in American history of all public college and university students in the state, after he had successfully convinced Texas Tech University administrators to require history of their students.[15]

Most Americans agreed with Haley that to win the battle against communism, American students needed to know US and Texas history. In 1953, US Senator William Jenner, who lead the Committee on the Judiciary's Subcommittee to Investigate the Administration of the Internal Security Act and other Internal Security Laws, explained in his report on "Subversive Influences in the Educational Process" that if subversive ideas were allowed in our schools, "not only will our youth be infused with seeds of their own and the Nation's destruction."[16]

Similar concerns were playing out in the Lone Star State. In May 1948, the State Board of Education meeting in Galveston expressed concerns over a history and geography textbook adoption because of the belief that the texts were opposed to "our way of life in the United States."[17] Just ten years later, another squabble over communist influences in Houston schools led Superintendent William Moreland to resign, and the school board inserted Houston and Texas history and geography in place of world history and geography, which prompted a former president of the University of Houston to declare that a "cotton curtain" was descending across the state. Defending the curricular changes, the new superintendent, a member of the White Citizens' Council, said the school board was "just drifting back to the fundamentals."[18] This was only the beginning, and within a few years, the most influential force in the Texas textbook wars emerged in East Texans Mel and Norma Gabler.

The Gablers, who became the most celebrated and feared of Texas textbook evaluators, lived in Hawkins in Wood County. By 1958 standards, they were not uneducated. She had a high school diploma and he had a year of college. They were initially troubled when their eldest son complained about his high school history textbook, Everette Augspurger and Richard A. McLemore's *Our Nation's Story*. As they looked into the textbook, the Gablers were surprised to find that the chapter on the American Constitution did not focus on states' rights or individual responsibility, but instead upon federal powers. They looked at American history books from 1885 and 1921, and in comparison found that the 1961 textbook had too much "modern" history. The new textbook did not have patriotic slogans of Patrick Henry's "Give me liberty, or give me death," nor Nathan Hale's regret about having only one life to give for his country, but was more interested in the United Nations.[19] They founded Educational Research Analysts to take advantage of the SBOE provision to allow public comments on textbooks before they came up for adoption.

Although not the first textbook critics in Texas, they started a successful grassroots campaign. One historian later commented that "the Gablers soon became the most recognized conservative voices among the petitioners." More importantly, the Gablers and their associates became a constant fixture at the SBOE textbook hearings for more than four decades. In addition to their persistence, "with the aid of extensive press coverage, the Gablers brought the anti-communist crusade to a new level in Texas education beginning in 1964."[20]

The Gablers were eager to challenge non-traditional family values, multiculturalism, un-Americanism, and—as the Supreme Court declared prayer and Bible reading in classrooms unconstitutional in 1962 and 1963—secular humanism. They were concerned that "Our basic American values are being thrown out the door" and maintained a constant vigil against what they perceived as ideological threats that attempted to influence Texas schoolchildren.[21]

The Gablers' tenacity and repeated appearances at Texas SBOE textbook hearings led them, and the organization they founded, to be the *sin qua non* gatekeeper for school textbook adoptions. The Gablers sometimes downplayed their influence. Norma Gabler once told William F. Buckley, Jr. in an interview for *The Firing Line*, "We have never had a vote on a textbook. So actually I don't know if we have... what effect we've had on it or not."[22] Educational historian Diane Ravitch explained, "Since the 1960s, any publisher that expected to win adoption of their textbooks in Texas had to anticipate that the Gablers would review the contents and values in their books and teachers' guides on a line-by-line basis." Despite their modesty, the Gablers were aware of their organization's strength and knew that their opposition to textbook adoptions would result in textual revisions to meet their demands.[23] Furthermore, within a few years they had become leaders in the conservative movement, and according to one report, "they achieved hero status in the eyes of thousands of concerned parents, fundamentalist religious leaders, and conservatives of the sort now identified with the New Right."[24] As I have previously written about the Gablers, "They were successful; they took a kitchen table project and created an organization, Educational Research Analysts, with a paid staff, which distributed materials for use to other concerned parents across the country. They were frequent guests on religious and national television news programs and became a significant force in the Religious Right."[25]

The Gablers' tremendous influence was their timing and organization. In 1960s Texas, there were ample reasons to believe that "traditional family values" were deteriorating. The rising threat of communism, immigration, Sputnik, threats to prayer in school, increased civil rights, rising divorce rates, legalized abortion, increased feminism, proliferation of drug use, and rock and roll music, many believed, threatened morality and challenged traditional American family values. In our nation's classrooms, students were being exposed to the "new math" and, it seemed, "a new history."

It is no wonder that movies like John Wayne's *The Alamo* (1960) resonated with American audiences. As one literature professor described, "Wayne's film is a conventional veneration of the heroic struggle for freedom by nineteenth-century frontiersmen, as a ragtag militia of soldiers and volunteers fight, against impossible odds, for self-determination and even the principle of a free Republic of Texas, as they face the tyrannical wrath of the mighty army of the despotic Mexican dictator General Antonio López de Santa Anna at a dilapidated fortress in San Antonio de Béxar in 1836."[26]

John Wayne made the story of the Alamo his personal quest for more than fourteen years. It cost $12 million to produce and used seven thousand extras. "I've got everything I own in it. I borrowed from banks and friends," Wayne told reporters. "But I'm not worried. This is a darn good picture. It's real American history, the kind of movie we need today more than ever."[27] But was it historical? One observer said that there was almost no scene in the movie based on any verifiable historical fact. Another scholar said, "historical truth can never be separated from its narration and interpretation, and most people, of course, know only or mainly the myths. It is almost always myths (or at least received and recycled versions of history) that shape our perception and therefore understanding of reality."[28] Don Graham explained, "*The Alamo* wasn't history; it was a sentimental ballad or, better yet, a sermon about freedom, the cold war, the concept of a republic, and a bunch of other Big Ideas that are in there somewhere. As Duke put it years later, 'There's more to that movie than my damned conservative attitude.'"[29] While the movie presents an almost ahistorical version of the Alamo, it recalls the heroic image of the past—"the cultural and spiritual values which we cherish so fondly; the blessed and romantic traditions of our glorious history"— embodied in the Texas Week declaration of the 1930s.

In one sense, people like the Gablers are early examples of modern-day school reformers. At one time, school reformers of the first half of the twentieth century were, as described by historian David Tyack, people "who wanted to create in the countryside the one best system that had been slowly developing in the cities." Yet, by the end of the twentieth century, it became commonplace to issue jeremiads against the public school system and its perceived failures. A new breed of reformers came forth who, instead of seeking to improve schools through consolidation, increased bureaucratization, and standardization, sought to return "local control" to the schools, and by that meant to bring a rural focus back to what they perceived as the over-centralization of the public school system.

Educational historian David Tyack writes that "book learning" was only one part of the education of young people that often took place in a larger community setting. "The child acquired his values and skills from his family and from neighbors of all ages and conditions. The major vocational curriculum was work on the farm or in the craftsman's shop or the corner store; civic and moral instruction came mostly in church or home or around the village where people met to gossip or talk politics. A child growing up in such a community could see work-family-religion-recreation-school as an organically related system of human relationships."[30] To the Gablers and others, however, instead of the community controlling schools, textbooks, and curriculums, these components of public education had been assumed by an impersonal, often distant, state board that approved textbooks published by New York companies.

The battle over how history is taught in public schools is a long struggle between modern and traditional interpretations of the past. The traditional, romantic version of the past found in the Texas Week Declaration of the 1930s, the *Texas History Movies* cartoons of the early twentieth century, or John Wayne's 1960s *The Alamo*, seek a simpler past. Chicago radio personality Paul Harvey once broadcast an essay written by Lee Pitts, the executive editor of *Livestock Market Digest*. The essay, "People Who Live at the End of Dirt Roads," yearns nostalgically for the "good old days" before paved roads. "What's mainly wrong with society today is that too many Dirt Roads have been paved. There's not a problem in America today, crime, drugs, education, divorce, delinquency that wouldn't be remedied, if we just had more Dirt Roads. . . ." The idea that things were simpler and more clear-cut in the past, as opposed the conflict and confusion of the present, is at the heart of the most traditional version of the past. Unfortunately, history is not as clean and simple as we want to believe. The tapestry of history is not of whole cloth. Upon close examination, we find the threads linking the elements of the past are incomplete, broken, and, more frequently than not, missing altogether. This is not because the fabric is old and tattered, but because the tapestry was fashioned out of incomplete cloth from the start. History is framed upon documentary sources, often missing and incomplete; around questions that are framed much later by people without a full understanding of the time they are studying, who arrive at answers influenced by present understanding. The design on the tapestry is therefore of necessity faint or imperceptible, and our efforts to discover the complete, full-color image is a knight's errand based more upon informed opinion than absolute certainly. The more research we do in the past, the more we learn about the past. Like the cartoon figure I mentioned at the beginning, for some people who were brought up on heroic images of past heroes, more recent versions of history might seem like a different history altogether.

Likewise, times have changed. In 2011, the 82nd Texas Legislature moved to limit powers of SBOE, perhaps as a result of the 2010 history standards battle. Senate Bill 6, introduced by Plano Republican Florence Shapiro, changed the policies regarding the SBOE's textbook adoptions. Instead of limiting funds for textbooks, school districts can now purchase other "instructional material"—a broad term—and the legislation ended a decades-long policy of the SBOE issuing lists of "conforming and non-conforming" texts. Previous to SB 6, school districts had to choose texts that "conformed" (met all the required curricular standards, or TEKS), or met at least fifty percent of the approved standards ("non-conforming"). SB 6 removed that requirement. Now, districts can determine whether the instructional materials they purchase with state allocated funds meet the TEKS.[31] Moreover, other states have refused to buy textbooks conforming to Texas's history standards, thus limiting the Lone Star State's power to influence the textbook industry. Even other conservative groups have criticized the Texas SBOE's attempts to impose a traditional romantic version of history. The current flap over the Advanced Placement History exam may backfire, as well. School districts have been pushing increasing number of students into AP courses in order to boost their numbers. This has resulted in a proportional decline in the number of students who actually receive AP credit that they can then use at in-state universities and colleges to bypass the six-hour

US/Texas history requirement. By rejecting the AP history exam, the SBOE will therefore force more college-bound students to take college/university-level history courses, where they will encounter the critical thinking requirements that the SBOE sought to have the students avoid in the first place.

In the end, however, challenges to the guardians of a traditional past are increasing, and recent successes such as the challenge over a hotly contested Mexican American Studies textbook have revealed that more modern interpretations of history are making inroads. The struggle will not end quickly, however. As one commentator put it, "In politics as in religion, Texans appear to have a low tolerance for difference. They are prepared to change but only like starlings, at the same time in the same direction and all at once."[32]

NOTES

1. David Ausubel, *Educational Psychology: A Cognitive View* (New York: Holt, Reinhart & Winston, 1968), p. vi.

2. Lauren McGaughy, "State, National Education Leaders Make AP Exam Changes," *Houston Chronicle*, September 17, 2014. Accessed October 2, 2014, www.houstonchronicle.com/news/education/article/State-national-education-leaders-makeAP-exam-5762936.php.

3. 2012 Republican Party of Texas, "Report of the Platform Committee," p. 12. Accessed 11/17/15 http://www.texasgop.org/wpcontent/themes/rpt/images/2012Platform_Final.pdf.

4. Eric Lach, "Texas GOP's 2012 Platform Opposed Teaching of 'Critical Thinking Skills'," *TPM*, June 29, 2012. Accessed 11/21/16, http://talkingpointsmemo.com/muckraker/texas-gop-s2012-platform-opposes-teaching-of-critical-thinking-skills?ref=fpb

5. Laura K. Munoz and Julio Noboa, "Hijacks and Hijinks on the US History Review Committee," in *Politics and the History Curriculum: The Struggle Over Standards in Texas and the Nation*, Keith A. Erekson, editor (New York, NY: Palgrave Macmillan, 2012), pp. 41-42.

6. Lance Fleming, "Textbooks Pass LISD Test Despite Concern Over Art," *Lubbock Avalanche Journal*, April 10, 1998. Accessed 9/23/14, http://lubbockonline.com/stories/041098/0410980041.shtml.

7. Gary B. Nash, Charlotte Crabtree, and Ross E. Dunn, preface to the Vintage Edition, *History on Trial: Culture Wars and the Teaching of the Past* (1997; reprint New York: Vintage Books, 2000), p. xiii.

8. *Ibid.*

9. Benjamin Fine, "Ignorance of U.S. History Shown By College Freshmen," *New York Times*, 4 April 1943.

10 "Texas Week," *Vernon's Texas Civil Statutes*, Title 106. Art. 6144a, Acts 1932, 42nd Leg., 3rd C.S., p. 131, S.C.R. No. 8. Accessed 9/28/14, https://www.tsl.texas.gov/ref/abouttx/txweek.html.

11. Don E. Carleton, *Red Scare!: Right-Wing Hysteria, Fifties Fanaticism, and Their Legacy in Texas* (Austin: Texas Monthly Press, 1985), 64 – 100.

12. "Non-Subversive Oath," attached to Chester E. Ollison, letter to Kenyon F. Clapp, 27 May 1970, "Subversive Oath (Textbook – Registrar

Book), Oaths," Texas Education Agency, Texas Education Agency Records, 1979/237-43, Texas State Library and Archives, Austin, TX.

13. James W. Fraser, *Between Church and State: Religion and Public Education in a Multicultural America* (New York: St. Martin's Griffin, 1999), pp. 142-149.

14. C. F. Schmidt, letter to editor, *Houston Chronicle*, 23 August 1957.

15. Anna L. Morales, "Repainting the Little Red Schoolhouse: The Texas American History Requirement and McCarthyism" (master's thesis, Texas Tech University, 1985), pp. 57–69.

16. Senate Judiciary Committee, Subcommittee to Investigate the Administration of the Internal Security Act and other Internal Security Acts, "Subversive Influences in the Educational Process," 83rd Cong., 1st sess., 1953, p. 2.

17. William M. Thornton, "Communist Adulation in Textbooks Blasted," *Dallas Morning News*, 11 May 1948.

18. "Education: Cotton Curtain," *Time*, 5 August 1957.

19 Eugene F. Provenzo, *Religious Fundamentalism and American Education: The Battle for the Public Schools* (Albany, NY: State University of New York Press, 1990), pp. 32-33.

20. Keith Alan Evetts, "The Gablers: Instigators or Products of Cold War Mentality in Texas" (Master's thesis, Baylor University, 1995), p. 24.

21. "Education: Was Robin Just a Hood?," *Time*, 31 December 1979.

22. "Issues Involved in Local Control of Reading Matter" program S0496 and transcript, recorded January 11, 1982, for broadcast on February 14, 1982, *Firing Line* (Television Program) Broadcast Records, Box 97, Hoover Institution Archives. Transcript accessed 9/24/2014 at http://hoohila.stanford.edu/firingline/displayTranscript.php?programID=917; video accessed 9/24/2014 at http://www.amazon.com/William-Buckley-Involved ControlReading/dp/B00BC44WG6 .

23. Diane Ravitch, *The Language Police: How Pressure Groups Restrict What Students Learn* (New York: Alfred A. Knopf, 2003), p. 105.

24. William Martin, "The Guardians Who Slumbereth Not," Texas Monthly, November 1982, accessed 15 March 2011, http://www.texasmonthly.com/1982=11=-1/feature.php

25. Gene B. Preuss, "'As Texas Goes, So Goes the Nation' Conservatism and Culture Wars in the Lone Star State," in *Politics and the History Curriculum: The Struggle over Standards in Texas and the Nation*, Keith A. Erekson, ed., (New York: Palgrave Macmillan, 2012), p. 29.

26. Philip Swanson, "Remember the Alamo? Mexicans, Texans and Americans in 1960s Hollywood," *Iberoamericana* 11, 44 (2011): p. 85.

27. Hector Saldana, "'The Alamo' Turns 50," *San Antonio Express-News*, October 23, 2010. Accessed 9/29/14, http://www.mysanantonio.com/entertainment/movies/article/The-Alamo-turns50-720600.php.

28. Swanson, "Remember the Alamo?," p. 90.

29. Don Graham, "Wayne's World," *Texas Monthly*, March 2000. Accessed 9/28/14, http://www.texasmonthly.com/story/wayne's-world/page/0/2.

30. David B. Tyack, *The One Best System: A History of American Urban Education* (Cambridge, MA: Harvard University Press, 1974), p. 15.

31. Janet Elliott, "AG Opinion Sought on Instructional Material for Schools," House Research Organization *Interim Brief*, August 11, 2015. Accessed 11/15/2016, https://txhronews.wordpress.com/2015/08/11/ag-opinion-sought-on-instructional-materials-forschools/.

32. Thomas Powers, "Texas: The Southern Baptists in Power," review of *Rough Country: How Texas Became America's Most Powerful Bible-Belt State* by Robert Wuthnow, *New York Review of Books*, October 9, 2014.

Bound for Beaumont: Eleanor Roosevelt's 1939 Train Trip Through East Texas and Beyond

Mary L Scheer

(It has long been the custom in our learned society—the East Texas Historical Association—for the departing president to address those assembled at the annual fall meeting in Nacogdoches. This talk, presented on October 9, 2015, represents a personal journey, from my research on Texas and Texas women to one more on the national stage. It is part of a larger project on Eleanor Roosevelt, who not only transformed the role of the first lady, but advocated for social justice, equality, and peace, making her a significant figure in her own right.)

Today, probably few people would associate the Roosevelt name, much less Eleanor Roosevelt, with East Texas or even Texas at large. She was born a Roosevelt; she was the niece of a Roosevelt, Teddy; and she was the wife of a Roosevelt—her fifth cousin, Franklin. All were patricians and from New York, a far distance from Texas. Born in 1884, Eleanor grew up to be a tall, shy, young woman who was intelligent, socially conscious, and a champion of the less fortunate. These qualities attracted her to Franklin, but their marriage was not close; it was essentially a political partnership, one that allowed Eleanor to develop her own independence, her own friendships, and her own interests.[1]

When she entered the White House in 1932, Eleanor Roosevelt thought of herself mostly as a teacher, having taught for several years at the Tod Hunter School, a small private academy for girls in New York City. Now, as First Lady, she had to give up teaching and wondered what she could do that was not the result "of somebody else's work and position." Eleanor turned naturally to speaking and writing, a choice that helped her navigate the world that she inherited. As a public speaker she adhered to the advice extended her by FDR's political advisor Louis Howe: "Have something to say, say it and sit down."[2]

In choosing to speak and write, Eleanor wanted to accomplish something meaningful with her life and, of course, there was a depression going on with real human need. There was also a mood of experimentation in the country to try to solve the crisis. Since her husband was confined to a wheelchair due to polio, she literally became his "eyes, ears, and legs" during the 1930s and 1940s. An astute observer, Eleanor became his proxy, a "publicist for the New Deal," as she traveled across the nation, making sure that federal agencies maintained their effectiveness and that the individual was never forgotten in the burgeoning bureaucracy.[3]

During her White House years, the first lady earned the nickname "Eleanor Everywhere." In addition to her normal schedule of sponsored radio talks, press conferences, newspaper columns, election campaigns, and White House duties, she also contracted with the management firm of W. Colston Leigh to make two lecture tours a year. Such a hectic, unprecedented pace for a first lady caught the attention of the editors of *Life* magazine. In 1940 they reported that since moving into the White House, Eleanor had traveled more than 280,000 miles, visited every state but South Dakota, shaken more than a half-million hands, given hundreds of lectures, and "probably not wasted as much time as the average person does in a week." In fact, she was on the road so much that one Washington news headline announced a rare occurrence. It read: MRS. ROOSEVELT SPENDS NIGHT AT WHITE HOUSE!"[4]

In March 1939, Eleanor Roosevelt embarked on one of her lecture tours, this time through the South and into Texas, for which she was paid $1,000 per speech. Now, working as a first lady was generally not standard behavior, but Eleanor Roosevelt was a non-traditional woman who just happened to be the president's wife. Earning her own money provided her with a sense of personal fulfillment and enabled her "to do many things for which her own income was insufficient." Further, she did not want "be a financial drain on her husband." So, beginning in 1935, she contracted every spring and fall to deliver speeches across the country on selected topics, ranging from social responsibility and the problems of youth to world peace and a typical day at the White House.[5]

Never a great public speaker, Eleanor Roosevelt became more comfortable on the public stage as time went on. She took elocution lessons to correct her high-pitched, shrill voice but was never satisfied with her performance. She suffered from nervousness and worried that people considered her as simply a "mouthpiece" for her husband. As an individual with opinions of her own, but also as the first lady, she had to walk a tightrope between her views and the official positions of her husband's administration. Despite her claims that FDR did not try to discourage or muzzle her, Eleanor never felt completely free to voice her own thoughts and opinions until she was out of the White House and on her own after 1945.[6]

As she began her lecture tour in 1939, the nation and the state were in a period of transition. Texas had benefited at the federal money trough in the 1930s, but the depression, although waning, was not yet resolved. Many of the New Deal reforms of the past six years had peaked and lost their crusading force. Events on foreign soil were now distracting

Texans from the large scale government spending programs to issues of isolationism, neutrality, and preparedness. Even President Roosevelt, in his annual State of the Union message to Congress in January 1939, said as much when he referred to the recent military aggression by Nazi Germany, fascist Italy and imperial Japan.[7]

Before the world dissolved into open hostilities, however, most Texans in early 1939 were still more concerned with day-to-day events at home than events abroad. With more than 300,000 Texans still out of work or on relief, they worried about the price of cotton, the continuation of public works jobs, and the stabilization of wages and taxes. Events such as the upcoming visit to the United States of King George VI and Queen Elizabeth of England, when the first lady dared to serve royalty hot dogs, and the announced retirement of Lou Gehrig, the great New York Yankee first baseman, after contracting a neuro-muscular disorder, grabbed national headlines. News about the invasions by Germany of Austria and Czechoslovakia, while condemned, seemed distant and none of their concern in the months before the outbreak of World War II in Europe.[8]

By 1939, the first lady was well versed with the issues facing Texans. Blessed with good health and energy, she was already a tireless traveler, crisscrossing the country and journeying thousands of miles. Eleanor had met and talked to those suffering from the depression across the nation. She had spoken out on controversial issues and openly supported new initiatives to solve some of the unjust situations she encountered. And she had filed detailed reports to her husband, particularly on the success or failure of many federal programs. As one *New York Times* reporter observed at the time, except for the president, she was "the best informed individual on the American scene."[9]

Eleanor Roosevelt began her three week-long train trip on March 6, 1939, accompanied by her secretary Malvina (Tommy) Thompson, nine small suitcases and "the inevitable knitting bag." Her route began in Washington, DC and would take her through the segregated Deep South, into Texas, and then westward to California. Opposed to the prevailing Jim Crow laws at the time, she had earlier committed an act of civil disobedience at the Southern Conference for Human Welfare in Birmingham, Alabama, by sitting on the "black side" of the meeting room. Further, Eleanor had resigned from the Daughters of the American Revolution (DAR) when black singer Marian Anderson was banned from Washington's Constitution Hall, controlled by the DAR. For these actions and others, she was both loved and hated in the South and had received death threats from the Ku Klux Klan. The reality in 1939, though, was that segregation policies were socially entrenched and legally enforced. She therefore reluctantly traveled by train in segregated train cars and spoke at segregated facilities as she moved throughout the South.[10]

The purpose of this 1939 train trip was three-fold: first, to deliver paid lectures to many places throughout the country to which she otherwise might never have gone; second, to report on New Deal programs to her husband "as a check against the many official reports he received;" and third, to keep the Roosevelt name and the administration's policies before the public. It was not all business, however, as she also found time for sightseeing and visiting family along the way.[11]

Fortunately, we know a lot about Eleanor's itinerary and thoughts through her syndicated newspaper column entitled "My Day," her own Bully Pulpit, which she wrote six days a week beginning in 1935 until her death in 1962. Many of her opinions, observations, and daily movements found their way into these columns. Written in a simple, matter-of-fact way, and in language that the average person could understand, no activity or subject was too humble or too lofty to report. For example, she wrote on a wide range of topics from gardening and childcare to human rights and politics. She also wrote about her travels and impressions of the people and the country during the Great Depression. From a historian's standpoint, these columns provide a valuable day-to-day, firsthand account of where she traveled, whom she met, and what issues, large and small, she encountered.[11]

Eleanor Roosevelt began the first leg of her trip, heading south through Virginia, Tennessee, Mississippi, and Louisiana, visiting local communities and inspecting New Deal programs. She gave public lectures at Natchez and Vicksburg, Mississippi. Her last stop before crossing into East Texas was at Baton Rouge, Louisiana. There, she visited Southern University in Scotlandville, just north of Baton Rouge, and toured a school for African-American children, headed by civil rights advocate Mary McLeod Bethune. This black education program was part of the National Youth Administration (NYA), a New Deal program that Eleanor Roosevelt directly championed and helped create. Aimed at youth, whom she called the "stranded generation," it provided job training for young people between the ages of sixteen and twenty-five who had dropped out of school and into a stagnating economy. At the time, though, the president was reluctant to add another federal relief program to the New Deal and he took a lot of convincing. Eleanor worked on him at the usual time for discussion of such questions—"right before he went to sleep." Preferring sleep to argument, the president eventually succumbed. On June 26, 1935, he signed executive order 7086 creating the NYA, which would also make a young twenty-six-year-old Lyndon Johnson the first NYA director in Texas. In 1939, it was this agency that was uppermost in her mind as she toured Texas and the South.[12]

As chief advocate and publicist for the NYA, Eleanor Roosevelt boarded the train in Baton Rouge on March 9, writing in her daily column that she was "bound for Beaumont." At every station along the way, people came to greet her, bringing flowers. Although outspoken and often controversial, she was still popular. In fact, the Gallup poll that year showed that the first lady outranked the president, winning sixty-seven percent approval compared to FDR's fifty-eight percent.[13]

Prior to arriving in Beaumont, a young female reporter, Merita Mills, joined Eleanor Roosevelt on the train in DeQuincy, Louisiana, for the ride to Beaumont. This followed the first lady's practice of holding female-only press conferences in the White House and meetings with women journalists in the field. She believed that it gave women journalists a chance they would not otherwise have received in a male-dominated profession. Obviously star struck by the first lady, Mills repeatedly referred to Mrs. Roosevelt as "my president's wife," and wrote that meeting the first lady was like "brushing against the flag." Engaged in friendly conversation as the Texas landscape slid by the train window, Mills asked the first lady what young women could do to serve their country. Eleanor answered by suggesting the remarkable work done in hospitals and government offices by the NYA, as well as civic and charitable organizations. If government would provide training for volunteers over a period of time, Eleanor advised, then young people could render "some service which would be of use to the communities in which they live."[14]

Eleanor Roosevelt crossed the Sabine River into Texas near Deweyville. She traveled through Mauriceville, a town of about 60 residents, and arrived in Beaumont, where a crowd of more than five thousand people greeted her. This was the first visit by a first lady to the city then or since. Disembarking at the Kansas City Southern Station in downtown Beaumont, she was welcomed by Mayor Ray Coale, along with members of the Altrusa Club, a local women's service organization. The Orange High School Bengal Guards then escorted her vehicle to the Hotel Beaumont, an eleven-story hotel constructed in 1922. There, she enjoyed a brief concert, followed by a short rest before beginning her day's event-filled agenda.[15]

Prior to her scheduled evening lecture, Eleanor Roosevelt met with NYA representatives from Jefferson County. She was "extremely interested" in their projects and learned about the county NYA training programs in woodworking, childcare, metalwork, and nursing. Students were also taught "to cook and make flags," and given job assistance. Roosevelt stressed that it was impossible for the NYA alone to fully solve the youth problem; it would require "the assistance of the people in the communities."[16]

"The Relation of the Individual to his Community" therefore became the theme of her lecture at the civic center that evening. Dressed in a long velvet gown, the first lady urged the audience to think about their responsibilities to their community. She advised that they should begin by studying their own neighborhoods and local government, and with that knowledge they could improve their lives not only at the local and state levels, but also in the nation and in the world. It was up to the individual to make democracy work, she emphasized, and "you can't say it is anybody else's business, because it is not; it is yours!"[17]

Following her lecture, the first lady customarily hosted a question and answer period, even taking questions meant to embarrass her. Here she could find out what was on the minds of her audience. While she generally tried to avoid politics, her audience did not. One question that evening from a Beaumonter was whether FDR would run for a third term. Due to the depression and possible war in Europe, many wondered if he would be a candidate again in 1940. She laughingly replied, "You'll have to ask him yourself. There are just some things one doesn't ask." Yet privately, Eleanor feared another four years in the White House. She worried about her husband's health, but also about the constraints placed on her as first lady. Additionally, there were many Americans constitutionally opposed to a third term, and some even suggested that Eleanor run instead and "Keep a Roosevelt in the White House!" Whenever the topic came up, however, she dismissed it, claiming that one president in the family was enough. Besides, she argued, she was too old and the country needed newer and younger leadership.[18]

Another pressing issue for many Texans at the time was the recent occupation of Austria and Czechoslovakia by Adolph Hitler. When questioned about the prospects for world peace, she stated that it divided into two distinct situations: the longtime view into the future and the immediate situation. "All you can do in the immediate situation is to look at it realistically and see what actually is going on and back whatever action seems to be most helpful at the time." A strong believer in disarmament, she eventually came to the painful realization that the U.S. would have to abandon its isolationism and neutrality. In the current situation, she stated, "we as a nation are foolish if we do not keep our arms up to a point where we can adequately defend ourselves." Since the president still publically pledged not to get involved in any foreign wars, Eleanor could say things as a trial balloon that the president could not. FDR, the consummate politician, could then weigh public reaction based on her probing comments and public reception.[19]

The next leg of her journey was from Beaumont to Fort Worth to spend the weekend with second son Elliott and his family. Unfamiliar with East Texas, she expected to see "a rather arid state." Instead, she saw green "fields which have evidently had more than their quota of rain." She made one brief stop at College Station, where Elliott was one of the trustees at Texas A&M College. There, she inspected resident NYA projects in agriculture and animal husbandry, catching a quick glimpse of the dairy and farm facilities before the train continued on.[20]

Arriving in Fort Worth on March 10 aboard the "Alamo," a special car attached to the Southern Pacific Railroad, she was met by her two-year-old grandson Elliott, Jr. and her daughter-in-law Ruth Roosevelt. Elliott, Sr., who was not always on good terms with his parents and eventually divorced four times, was in New York and unable to be present. He owned and operated several radio stations (Texas State Network) and often disagreed publicly with his parents over a third term for his father, American intervention in Europe, and her mother's friends in the American Youth Congress, a suspected communist organization. In fact, that was one reason why Eleanor Roosevelt had one of the largest FBI files at the time. Nevertheless, she looked forward to seeing her son, daughter-in-law, and two grandchildren on his Texas ranch. Her crowded schedule included an interview at a radio station, a discussion with "two gentlemen from the NYA," and then a train ride to Abilene for a speaking engagement on "A Day at the White House" at Hardin-Simmons University. This hectic pace left everyone but Eleanor breathless.[21]

On March 13, Eleanor left Fort Worth by car to travel to Sherman. Again, she was scheduled to give a public lecture, this time to the Texas League of American Pen Women, a woman's club to promote female creative activities. While in route, a dust storm erupted, but her driver assured her that "we never have any bad ones in this part of the State." That was not the case, though, and the storm proved to be "the worst they had seen." Visibility was limited and the car had "to stop once or twice because we could not see the road ahead very clearly." This firsthand experience of the effects of the Dust Bowl convinced the first lady of the need for soil conservation programs in regions without rain for so long. In her column the next day, she wrote, "There is no doubt that much of the country which has been put under cultivation should go back into grass and be used as range for cattle."[22]

Returning to the Roosevelt ranch, Eleanor had time to visit with Elliott and catch up with the family. Later that evening they attended the Southwestern Exposition and Stock Show in Fort Worth with Texas Governor and Mrs. O'Daniel. Her first experience at "a real rodeo," impressed Eleanor. Being an equestrian herself, she appreciated the cowboys' ability to ride and their "strength and agility in dealing with cattle." Eleanor's overall impression of the region was stereotypical—she called it "cowboy country," where even in the larger cities, Texans are conscious of "the picturesqueness of this part of their population."[23]

After three very busy days, Eleanor Roosevelt said goodbye to her grandchildren and left Fort Worth for Houston. This third leg of her trip was first by car and then by train. Driving with Elliott and wife Ruth, they first stopped at Hillsboro to see "a practice house for girls." This NYA facility was an innovative school for rural girls to attend for two weeks and then return home for two weeks to put into practice what they learned, and then the cycle would repeat. Arriving in Waco to meet the train, Eleanor had time to inspect a building constructed at the municipal airport by the NYA boys and meet with the NYA State Advisory Committee. After a brief rest, she then boarded the train, arriving in Houston the next day.[24]

In 1939, Houston was a town of about 375,000 residents where, with the help of private banks and welfare agencies, the depression came later and left earlier than other parts of the nation. As was her custom, before she disembarked from the train she met the public and press on the train platform for a brief speech. Later, in her Rice Hotel suite, she held a press conference, followed by a tour of Jefferson Davis Hospital, where NYA girls held jobs. Accompanied by J. C. Kellam, state NYA supervisor, and Houston director W. O. Alexander, she traveled to a rural school in Cypress and talked with NYA boys building a house for the school superintendent, to Hempstead to inspect a new community center, and then to Prairie View College, the only state supported black college, to inspect NYA dormitories. The day ended with a reception and an evening lecture at Sam Houston Coliseum.[25]

Following her brief Houston stay, Eleanor Roosevelt left East Texas to continue her journey. On this fourth leg of her tour, she drove to the Rio Grande Valley, a region known for its citrus fruits and vegetables. Arriving in Edinburg on her first visit to this part of the state, she wrote in her daily column that the area resembled "Southern California or in Florida." After a brief crossing into Mexico, she toured Engleman Gardens, a ranch of about 11,000 acres, and viewed citrus groves and a packing plant. She also drove through Weslaco, where an experimental station was "developing various new usages for the products of the valley." The next morning, March 17, was the thirty-fourth anniversary of her marriage to FDR. With no mention of it in her "My Day" column, she drove to Harlingen, "paralleling the line of the Southern Pacific Railway." Along the way, she viewed the Rio Grande that supplied the essential water supply to the region. Reflecting her own philosophy to see things for herself, she observed, "In this big country of ours we have to see things with our own eyes to realize the things which may spell ruin to the entire section and yet which mean so little in other parts of the country."[26]

Leaving the valley on March 18, Eleanor Roosevelt arrived by train to San Antonio, the fifth leg of her journey. Accompanied by Mayor Maury Maverick, his wife, and Mrs. Harry Drought, she visited local industries and historical sites. Always a staunch supporter of labor, especially women in the workforce, Eleanor was keenly interested in the needlework industry and the conditions of its female workers. The real difficulties, she observed, were not in union shops, but in the home garment work done outside organized industry. Other concerns were the replacement of handmade goods by machines and the high tuberculosis rate in the city.[27]

Along with her visits to local industries, Eleanor also found time to visit the old Spanish Governor's Palace, "a beautiful piece of restoration," the Witte Museum, where a pioneer log cabin was being built by the NYA boys, and several WPA projects. Afterwards, she boarded the train for the last leg of her journey.[28]

Eleanor Roosevelt's last day in Texas was spent riding the rails along "miles and miles of desert" through West Texas. Looking out her window the next morning, she saw "a few cattle, some goats and some sheep with their lambs," moving about. Crossing the Pecos River Bridge, she gazed down into the 381-foot canyon. She passed dry arroyo beds and small ranch houses. As she crossed into New Mexico heading for California, she looked forward to visiting daughter Anna and son-in-law John, who were expecting their first child. But before leaving the state, she reflected on her impressions of crisscrossing Texas and talking to its citizens:

> These people are all conscious of the riches of the state in which they live. They know that there are vast natural resources still undeveloped. They know that they grow certain things at a day [and] time when a ready market is to be found in other state.[sic] However, you hear one complaint from them: "Why can't we get action from the Interstate Commerce Commission

and Congress in the matter of freight rate differentials?"[29]

This three-week train trip to East Texas and beyond was both ordinary and extraordinary. It was ordinary because it demonstrated Eleanor Roosevelt's genuine interest in the common man. By seeking out a cross section of people, she wanted to ensure that the New Deal relief agencies served the most needy and neglected groups, including blacks, women, and sharecroppers. She also spoke in a simple language to ordinary men and women about their day-to-day concerns during the waning years of the Great Depression. She learned about all manner of issues and problems that affected Texans, from the lack of rain and loss of jobs to needlework and even freight rate differentials. Her unassuming manner and sincerity convinced people that she cared about their problems and would use her influence and access to power to try and correct injustices. Her appeal, though, was not based solely on her relationship with the president. Audiences were enchanted with her personality, her directness, her humanitarianism, her warmth, and her unselfish interest in people. Her adversaries as well as her friends acknowledged this.

At the same time, this trip was extraordinary in the sense that the first lady, initially a shy and submissive young woman and wife, could carve out a public role for herself other than official hostess at the White House. Her experiences and travels certainly did not fit into the standard role for first ladies. No other first lady before or since could match her energy, public service, or concern for the downtrodden. Her lecture tours took her to places such as East Texas to see firsthand the needs of the people. Never elected to public office, Eleanor acted as an intermediary between the average citizen and the government. Her trip was also remarkable in that she traveled without the use of the secret service or police escorts. In fact, she refused to be trailed by secret service agents. Only after she demonstrated the ability to protect herself with a concealed gun that she carried did the secret service agency acquiesce in her going without their protection. As humorist Will Rogers observed about Eleanor, who often traveled alone, "No maid, no secretary—just the First Lady of the land on a paid passenger ticket" to somewhere.[30]

Ultimately, Eleanor's 1939 train trip to East Texas and beyond expanded the image of the first lady, promoted the New Deal agenda, and exerted political influence on the administration. It also was a platform to understand the needs of the forgotten man and woman during the depression and throw light on such programs as the NYA, which she championed. But historians and others disagree on her significance and effectiveness. Was she a busybody, as some thought, or a political insider and confidant of the president? Should a first lady work for pay or be expected to volunteer for certain causes? Did she neglect her family by her frequent absences or provide a needed service for her disabled husband? Was she a humanitarian reformer or a radical who threatened the foundations of American society? Did she exercise political power or feminine influence to pursue her own social causes? While Eleanor Roosevelt always denied that she exerted any political influence on her husband or anyone else in government, saying that she was just passing along requests or suggestions that came to her, the historical record tells another story. What we can say is that Eleanor Roosevelt was one of the most controversial and influential women in Washington, and her 1939 train trip through East Texas and beyond allowed her to play a key role in connecting the public to the government during the worst years of the Great Depression.

NOTES

1. There is a large amount of Roosevelt historiography, both of Franklin and Eleanor. Several good sources on Eleanor include: Joseph P. Lash, *Eleanor and Franklin* (New York: New American Library 1971, reprint 1973); Blanche Wiesen Cook, *Eleanor Roosevelt*, 2 vols. (New York: Viking, 1992; 1999); Tamara Hareven, *Eleanor Roosevelt: An American Conscience* (Chicago: Quadrangle Books, 1968); Hazel Rowley, *Franklin and Eleanor: An Extraordinary Marriage* (New York: Farrar, Straus and Giroux, 2010); Joseph P. Lash, *Eleanor, The Years Alone* (New York: New American Library, 1972); Joan Hoff-Wilson, *Without Precedent: The Life and Career of Eleanor Roosevelt* (Bloomington: Indiana University Press, 1984). Eleanor also wrote her autobiography, *This I Remember* (New York: Harper & Brothers, 1949).

2. Speeches and articles, 1934, Eleanor Roosevelt Papers Franklin Roosevelt Presidential Library, Hyde Park, New York, hereinafter cited as ER Papers. Lash, *Eleanor and Franklin*, p. 553.

3. Lash, *Eleanor and Franklin*, pp. 551-570.

4. Emblidge, ed., *My Day, 1936-1962*, p. 43.

5. Eleanor frequently donated her radio and lecture fees to charity, especially to the American Friends Service Committee. Lash, *Eleanor and Franklin*, p. 555; Eleanor Roosevelt Biography, National First Ladies' Library, pp. 12-13, www.firstladies.org/biographies/firstladies.aspx?biography=33, accessed August 10, 2015.

6. Roosevelt, *This I Remember*, p. 152; ER to L.Hickock, April 19, 1945, ER Papers; Eleanor Roosevelt Biography, p. 12.

7. Franklin D. Roosevelt, State of the Union Address, January 2, 1939, Washington, DC.

8. Eleanor Roosevelt, *The Autobiography of Eleanor Roosevelt* (Boston: G.K. Hall & Co., 1937), pp. 199-207; Robert A. Calvert, Arnoldo De León, and Gregg Cantrell, *The History of Texas*, third edition (Wheeling, Illinois: Harlan Davidson, 2002), p. 320.

9. David Emblidge, ed., *My Day, 1936-1962* (Boston: Da Capo Press, 2001), p. 34.

10. Eleanor Roosevelt, "My Day," February 27, 1939, in Emblidge, ed., *My Day*; Eleanor Roosevelt, "My Day," March 7, 1939, Eleanor Roosevelt Papers, George Washington University, Washington, DC, hereinafter referred to as "My Day;" *Fort Worth Star-Telegram*, March 10, 1939; James MacGregor Burns and Susan Dunn, *The Three Roosevelts: Patrician Leaders who Transformed America* (New York: Grove Press, 2001), p. 394; Allida M. Blck, *Casting Her*

Own Shadow: Eleanor Roosevelt and the Shaping of Postwar Liberalism (New York: Columbia University Press, 1996), pp. 40-44; Cook, *Eleanor Roosevelt*, p. 436.

11. Emblidge, ed., My Day, p. xi.

12. Roosevelt, "My Day," March 7-9, 1939; Carol A. Weisenberger, *Dollars and Dreams: The National Youth Administration in Texas* (New York: Peter Lang, 1994), pp. 16-19; "National Youth Administration," *The Handbook of Texas Online*, tshaonline.org/handbook/online/articles/ncn04, accessed September 5, 2015.

13. Roosevelt, "My Day," March 9, 1939; Emblidge, ed., *My Day*, p. 33; Gallup Poll, 1939.

14. *Beaumont Enterprise*, March 9, 1939; Roosevelt, "My Day," March 10, 1939.

15. *Ibid.*

16. Robert W. Touchet, "New Deal Work Programs in Jefferson County, Texas: The Civilian Conservation Corps at Tyrrell Park," MA thesis 1972, Lamar University, Beaumont, TX; *Beaumont Enterprise*, March 9, 1939; Roosevelt, "My Day," March 10, 1939.

17. *Beaumont Enterprise*, March 9, 1939.

18. *Ibid*; Joseph P. Lash, *Love Eleanor: Eleanor Roosevelt and Her Friends* (Garden City, NY: Doubleday and Co., 1982), pp 280 and 319-320.

19. *Beaumont Enterprise*, March 9, 1939.

20. Roosevelt, "My Day," March 10-11, 1939; Burns and Dunn, *The Three Roosevelts*, pp. 311-312.

21. Roosevelt "My Day," March 11, 1939.

22. Roosevelt, "My Day," March 14, 1939.

23. Roosevelt, "My Day," March 13, 1939; *Fort Worth Star-Telegram*, March 10, 1939.

24. Roosevelt, "My Day," March 15, 1939.

25. The census of 1940 listed 384,514 residents in Houston. *Houston Post-Dispatch*, March 12, 14-15, 1939; *Houston Chronicle*, March 15, 1939; Roosevelt, "My Day," Marh 15, 1939.

26. Roosevelt, "My Day," March 16-17, 1939.

27. Roosevelt, "My Day," March 18-19, 1939.

28. *Ibid.*

29. Roosevelt, "My Day," March 20, 1939.

30. Eleanor typically only carried a pistol when she was alone in a car. Cook, *Eleanor Roosevelt*, p. 436; Eleanor Roosevelt Biography, p. 15; Rogers, quoted by Burns and Dunn, *The Three Roosevelts*, p. 268.

The Long Journey of Joshua Louis Hicks:
A Voice from the Texas Working Class

Kyle Wilkison

Joshua Louis Hicks (1857-1921) spent over half his working life investing the hard labor and reaping the sparse rewards of a late nineteenth century American farm laborer and farmer, that condition made worse by being in the South, most especially East Texas. He occupied his last two decades as a print shop worker and typesetter. The day he died, he was a dues-paid-up-card-carrying member of the Waco Typographical Union, No. 188, a local within the International Typographical Union. As a twenty-three-year-old farmer, Hicks found his voice in 1880 writing columns, editorials, and letters published in local and regional newspapers, usually in defense of Prohibition. The rate of these contributions increased as his interests shifted to the Farmers Alliance, Populist and Socialist parties and his writings appeared in the pages of the organs of those movements. At various times he wrote regular editorials and features for the *Dallas Laborer*, the *Dallas Craftsman*, the *West Texas Sentinel*, the *Farmers' Journal*, the *Dallas Pitchfork* and the *Texarkana Socialist*. He contributed reports, poems, features and letters to the *Christian Advocate*, the *Advocate-Advance*, *Hopkins County Echo*, the *Abilene Reporter*, the *Dallas News*, the *Waco Times Herald*, the *Waco Tribune*, the *Union Advance* and the *Sulphur Springs Gazette*. This is not an exhaustive listing.

Hicks's writings reveal the passion of an idealist often at odds with the cruel vagaries of the world and his own culture. They also reveal the questing mind of a voracious reader. His willingness to question all sorts of authority supplied a tempering skepticism that led him to re-examine beliefs throughout his life and adjust his conclusions over time. He began his writing life as a zealous Prohibitionist and primitive Christian. Near the end, he had abandoned both Prohibition (ironically just as it was winning the day) and formal religion. Yet, some things did not change over his forty-year odyssey (1880-1921) of public writings: Hicks hated violence and war, denounced white supremacy, supported female suffrage, and, eventually, longed for a Socialist commonwealth.[1]

Some might suggest that a white East Texas farmer and working man who believed these things must have been an outlier, even one-of-a-kind. While obviously fascinating to historians, is not he otherwise insignificant in understanding the mainstream history of this place? Why should we care about Hicks and his unusual worldview?

As Lawrence Goodwyn, James R. Green, and Chandler Davidson have shown, agrarian radicals like Hicks formed a substantial minority in the late-nineteenth and early-twentieth-century Southwest. But, in our stronger-than-history cultural memory, such people have been categorically erased and replaced by cowboys, oilmen, entrepreneurs and other iconic myths more serviceable to contemporary elites. Consequently, we think we know more about the poor majority, the American, and Texas, and East Texas working class than we really do. Such people appear as stock villains in our popular culture from the facile stereotyping of the entertainment industry to the uninformed generalizations of pundits and even scholars. Indeed, they remain the butt of the last safely expressed public bigotry in mainstream American culture. Writing a 2016 election-year piece in the *National Review*, political pundit Kevin D. Williamson explained the poverty of the twenty-first century American working class (including those in his native Texas), with the same contemptuous language used by Hicks' opponents a century earlier. In spite of the fact that "nothing happened to them," Williamson writes, he finds them filled with "an incomprehensible malice." Far from being victims of "the Man," the working class is poor because it is dysfunctional, dependent, and engages in the "whelping of human children with all the respect and wisdom of a stray dog." Such characterizations could have come from the press of Gilded Age Texas seeking to explain the rise of rural poverty during the agricultural crises of the 1880s and 1890s. Indeed, as Nancy Isenberg's important 2016 work, *White Trash: The 400-Year Untold History of Class in America* shows, the roots of such contempt for the poor majority run even further back into American history. In all times and places in the American past, spokespersons for the elite have explained disparities of wealth as the natural result of the distribution of virtue within a population using the reigning normative language of the age: religion, science, economic ideology, or, more recently, a sort of pop-ethnography that finds a "culture in crisis." In every era the economic winners have confidently explained that the working poor majority ("hillbillies," "white trash," "rednecks," "black rednecks," "losers" or worse) embodied backward traits that kept them poor.[2]

What follows is the brief story of a poor man, a small farmer and hourly wage hand in newspaper print shops. Nevertheless, within this small story lie big contradictions of the malicious cultural portraits we have come to accept for the poor and working class. We would know nothing of this obscure—if prolific—member of the working class if not for his diligence in preserving his published pieces in scrapbooks and handing them down to Louis Hicks—his labor activist son—who preserved them. It was then history's good fortune that led him in 1977 to George N. Green, of the University of Texas at Arlington, one of the founding fathers of Texas labor history, who saw to the preservation of the Hicks Family Papers in UT-Arlington's Texas Labor Archives.[3]

Joshua Louis Hicks was born in 1857, the oldest of four children in southwestern Alabama on a small family farm in a county of small semi-subsistence farms. When Hicks was six-years-old, his father died leaving Hick's mother Nancy to provide for the young family. A family friend described Nancy Hicks as "full of humility and love" and "free of prejudice or bigotry." She must have been a hard worker, too. Somehow, she kept the family intact and on the farm, probably with the help of kin, for another decade. Hicks described it as a hard childhood but wrote glowingly of his mother. His mother was a member of a religious minority—a Primitive Baptist—in a county noted for another religious minority—a small colony of Quakers—and it is tantalizing to note that this woman's youngest son was named William Penn Hicks. According to the census records, in 1860 they had been among the respectable poor majority with seven hundred dollars worth of land and no slaves. By the following decade, this fatherless family's fortunes had dropped by over half and they were looking to get out of Alabama. At age eighteen, Joshua struck out for Texas working as a plow hand and cotton picker in Brazos County.[4]

By 1880, the widow Nancy Hicks, along with her three grown sons and married daughter, lived together on a homeplace in Hopkins County, Texas, which lies in the beautiful Post Oak strip with its magnificent hardwood trees, sun-dappled meadows, and cheap sandy soil. Such soil would produce all the subsistence a family could want as long as they never needed money. Taxes, mortgages, doctors, and the like demanded cash, but small farmers could pay with the proceeds from the money crop of cotton, which would indeed grow there but sparsely and under protest. The Hicks family lived in the euphoniously named community of Forest Academy, about ten miles from the county seat of Sulphur Springs. It is instructive that the census-taker labeled Nancy Hicks and her three adult sons as illiterates in the 1880 census. Within a few months of the visit, the supposedly illiterate Joshua Hicks made his debut in the pages of the East Texas press as a gifted writer, and his two younger brothers would exhibit similar levels of literary competence. How did the census-taker arrive at his assessment of the Hicks boys' literacy? Might he have been estimating the value of their farm, their economic status, their class, instead?[5]

Joshua Hicks turned twenty-three years old the year of the census. He had put in his time as a farmhand to get his family to Texas and buy land, and he was living in a growing community that included young women. His thoughts turned to love. And, by that I mean the sappy, gob-smacked, doggerel-writing variety addressed to 19-year-old Henrietta Elizabeth Harrison, "the girl I love so dear," with whom he would spend the next fifty years: "In dream of night I oft-times view those lovely smiles so sweet; then when I wake my all I'd give to see those rosy cheeks."[6] His writing improved with time. In any case, apparently Henrietta liked this poem as well as his carefully handwritten marriage proposal. They married when she was twenty-one, and together they had eight children.[7]

During the decade he spent farming at Forest Academy, Hicks began writing contributions to the newspaper in the county seat of Sulphur Springs with reports on the doings of the farm folk of his community. He subscribed to, or at least read, a variety of local newspapers as well as national papers promoting Prohibition and agrarian reform. Along the way, he became a zealous partisan of Prohibition and occasional defender of the agrarian ideal. His range of contributions widened to include pieces in the regional Prohibition and Granger newspapers he read. He stuck mainly to prose with occasional returns to what he called poetry. With each passing piece, his writing achieved greater ease and confidence, revealing an earnest and occasionally eloquent voice. This period is also when he first challenged conventional stereotypes. During his zealous defense of the Prohibition Party, he regularly denounced the hold that Civil War memory and resentment played in maintaining Southern white voters' loyalty to the Democratic Party.

In 1882, Hicks turned out what was, perhaps, his best poem and was rewarded by seeing it appear in the Mississippi state Granger newspaper. It read, in part:

> How strange! When farmers every hour
> Feel the death-grip of corp'rate power
> They do not rally to the Grange—
> Their only hope. Is this not strange?
> How strange! That Congressmen should pass
> Bills in behalf of every class
> Except farmers; to them they cry,
> "You need no help." (Root, hog, or die.)
> How strange! That some who advocate
> Religion in the Lone Star State
> Should be so deaf to human cries
> As to publish the railroads' lies.[8]

What followed this in the 1880s is a long string of essays defending, promoting, and preaching the Prohibition Party line. It is within the reams of that dry discourse that Hicks wrote something brave and unexpected. He took on Texas' leading Prohibition luminary, the formidable Rev. Dr. J. B. Cranfill, publisher of Texas Baptists' prohibition newspaper and financial secretary of Baylor University.[9]

In an 1888 editorial carried by a nationwide Prohibitionist newspaper, Cranfill furiously warned Northern Prohibitionists to "abandon all that nonsense about 'breaking down the color line.'" In a following issue, Hicks took his stand. He approached the question carefully, claiming the Northerners meant only to eliminate the color line politically, not socially. The Northern reformers simply "see no good reason why the two races should stand arrayed against each other at the ballot-box. That such is the case here in the south no-one [sic] can deny. And that it results from the war—is a fruit gathered from old battlefield's [sic], which is poisonous and destructive to the political health of this nation, cannot be seriously questioned." Hicks defended the only somewhat less incendiary position that Northerner Prohibitionists thought black and white Southerners should ignore race in their voting behavior and that "they are right about it, until some decent reason is shown why the whites and blacks in the south should vote against each other." "How like a wet blanket" Cranfill's rejection must be "upon the ardent zeal of Bishop Turner, Hector Jordan and other colored men who are laboring and suffering and sacrificing for the uplifting of their race—and our own."[10]

Cranfill was unmoved. "With my own eyes," he retorted days later, "in the Northern states I have seen negro [sic] and white children attending the same school, playing on the same playground, and those same children recited together in the same classes." From there, he warned, "it is but a step to intermarriage" and "race annihilation and the end of the Anglo-Saxon." Cranfill reminded his readers that he had said before and continued to maintain that "the negro is a lower race . . . that he is not . . . the equal of the white man and will never be."[11]

Hicks did not reply. Indeed, after this famous preacher's rebuke, he went silent on race for years. In 1915, he wrote in the *American Socialist* that Southerners needn't dread that Socialism would be the catalyst to erase the color line because capitalism had already achieved that. Somewhat tongue-in-cheek Hicks described black and white workers digging together in the same ditch and black and white businessmen filing deeds in the same courthouse with the observation that capitalism had already achieved what white Southerners accused Socialists of seeking to do.[12]

Hicks gets close to, but did not arrive at, values many on the left hold dear in our own time. He did not live in our time. He lived in Waco, in 1916, where white men burned a seventeen-year-old African American child to death on the courthouse lawn and then brought their own children to see his charred remains. Over a year after his neighbors tortured and murdered young Jesse Washington, Hicks ventured forth in the local paper with a column entitled "When the Mob Gets Started." He carefully stated that he based this column on his reading of a sociology tome that analyzed mob mentality and on a sickening experience from his own youth. "When you read the book you will get an idea of how quickly the human animal can descend from heights divine and be drawn into a mob and do things, as a member of the mob, that he could not be hired to do on his own moral responsibility as an individual." He then related a disturbing experience from his young farmhand days in Brazos County. One snarling, howling, shrieking night he lay in bed and listened in dread as the otherwise friendly neighborhood dogs ganged up on and killed a stray dog wandering into the community. After describing in gruesome detail the blood-chilling sounds he heard that night, he told his Waco readers: "The noise I heard was the noise of a mob."[13]

Hicks did not arrive at class-consciousness in a sprint. It took over a decade of struggle as a small farmer for him to show signs of beginning such a journey. Through his many writings in the 1880s and 1890s, we can observe that beginning. In his twenties, he followed the conventional New South line that diversification and frugality would save the small farmer. While acknowledging that the new year of 1885 brought cries of "'hard times,'" debt and "'short crops,'" Hicks insisted that if only farmers would reform themselves, diversify and "live at home" their "state of affairs would be alleviated."[14] The oft-repeated phrase "live at home" was a nineteenth-century phrase that would persist well into the twentieth century and used generally to pass judgment on farmers who supposedly spent too much money at the credit merchant's store for sustenance, which they could have grown in their own garden patch.

A year later, on January 16, 1886, found Hicks still blaming his fellow farmers for widespread rural poverty. He rejected the agrarian radicals' charge that railroad and corporate collusion explained cotton farmers' distress. Instead, he blamed the "credit system," or, more accurately, farmers who relied upon credit. The twenty-nine-year-old counseled greater self-restraint and to stop visiting the merchant unless one had something to trade or sell. "That's the route for me though the bridge over the next eight months be ever so shaky."[15]

In the spring of 1886, he took on the Farmers' Alliance plan for cooperative "Exchange Stores," which he feared would run honest merchants out of business. Once Alliance Exchange Stores were the only supplier available, Hicks predicted they would gouge farmers as badly as any privately held monopoly. He sparred with a correspondent from neighboring Reilly Springs in the *Hopkins County Echo* over the virtues of frugality and greater competition versus the pitfalls of cooperation through the Farmers' Alliance. While Hicks claimed to agree with much of the Alliance program, he feared the "misguided zeal and blind prejudice" of the "average farmer" would ruin what good was in it and warned once more about putting small town merchants out of business. Once more asserting his faith in competition, he declared that farmers "need a thousand more merchants in Sulphur Springs" not fewer. The only worthy object of the Farmers' Alliance was to educate farmers on scientific agriculture and the evils of credit accounts.[16]

It took three more years of the increasingly deflationary 1880s cotton market to chasten the young farmer. Then in his thirties and with a wife expecting their fifth child, a considerably humbled Hicks wrote a column for the local paper lamenting "honest debts." How to make a bale of cotton pay:

> store accounts, bank notes, doctors' and druggists' bills, taxes, [and] etc. . . . is the knottiest, stubbornest, and most harassing question that ever drove sleep from the eyes of an honest farmer. It makes him almost insensible to the needs of his family. It rises like a black mountain before his eyes whenever he looks forward and tries to plan for the future. It makes him utter groans that can be understood only by honest men, who have contracted honest debts and who have made all honest endeavors to meet those debts, and have failed. It harrows the very soul, and drives one sometimes to the verge of dementia.

After laying out the deplorable conditions assailing the entire agricultural community, and showing genuine empathy for the farmers' creditors who would not be fully paid, Hicks uncharacteristically articulated temporary defeat. "This is not written," he admitted, "with any purpose of offering a remedy." Then he added grimly, "I shall remedy my part of it sooner or later, in the providence of God."[17]

This was a pivotal moment for Hicks and his young family. He heard the railroad companies' siren song of the west central rolling plains around Abilene and abandoned the beautiful if un-remunerative Post Oak strip for Taylor County, a place where mesquite bushes were often mistaken for trees. They arrived in Abilene in the dead of winter

1891, when Henrietta Elizabeth, she of the sweet smile and rosy cheeks, immediately gave birth to their sixth child. The thirty-four-year-old Hicks soon discovered that Taylor County land sold only by the section. He tried to convince his new neighbors that Abilene would never prosper until landowners were willing to sell smaller parcels to "the fifty acre man" whose tilling of the soil surely "would invite rain" and lead to prosperity. Unfortunately for him, that purported connection between plowing and raining was one of the "railroads' lies" that he missed.[18]

The move to Taylor County was not the only big change on Hicks' horizon. He was now a true believer in the Alliance all the way to the Subtreasury Plan, the litmus test for Texas radicals. His understanding of the currency deflation then killing farmers and debtors had increased as well, but with characteristic optimism, he thought he saw relief on the horizon through the building of a new "formidable" political party: "All money has increased in value, all labor has decreased in value, wages have been reduced; all prices have been brought down, and debts are doubly hard to pay. And the country will not stand the contraction, and henceforth a formidable party is being built up, which is seeking and demanding relief."[19] Hicks and his Alliance district voted to send their representative to St. Louis to the founding convention of the People's Party and in support of all of the "Ocala Demands" as written.[20]

Of the many varieties of 1890s populists, Hicks was of the capital-P variety, meaning he saw the silverite derangement as the "shadow movement" it was and cleaved to the leftist "midroaders" and Subtreasury men, denouncing the folly of Bryan and fusion. In another change from the last decade, Hicks started to note what he considered bad behavior by preachers in their betrayals of the interests of the poor majority in favor of their wealthy supporters. In fact, he charged that the Taylor County pulpit was "almost [as] a unit against political reforms."[21]

For Hicks the Populists were the true democrats, the true heirs of Jefferson, not the plutocrats of the moment running the Texas and national Democratic Party. As a good propagandist, he reported that the Populists had "about captured" his district and that an uncle in Greer County reported "the People's party is practically solid in that section."[22]

The more Hicks studied the Populist Party and the agrarian malaise to which it responded, the better he liked the party and the less he liked farming. From his early adulthood, he had maintained a special connection to newspapers and their editors. By learning the printer's trade, Hicks solved his personal farm problem while simultaneously slaking his thirst for the world of newspapers, more particularly a Populist newspaper, Abilene's *West Texas Sentinel*. Occasionally, Hicks even got to write for the newspaper he printed. Having written steadily for more than twelve years for no pay, it must have been a thrill to be on a newspaper team, even from the back of the shop. This would be Hicks' lifetime career. No matter his obvious talent and growing eloquence, he spent the rest of his life in the blue-collar end of journalism.[23] In any case, the Populist Party and its newspapers did not outlast the decade, and by late summer 1899, the forty-two-year-old father of eight sought and found employment printing the *West Texas Baptist*.[24]

Just before Hicks found work with the Baptists, the United States government declared war on Spain. Like people in many small towns and cities across Texas, Abileneans rallied their boys and young men to the colors in recruiting campaigns sometimes led by local pastors. Joshua Hicks would have no part of this conjoining of Christianity and nationalist zeal. Indeed, outraged at the prospect of preachers recruiting for war, he wrote and published a pamphlet denouncing their role—and any Christian's role—in the war effort. It was Hicks' position that no Christian might fight in a war and "shoot down his fellow-man" without contradicting the central message of Christ. Arguing from a Christian quietist-pacifist perspective--similar to the Amish but much at odds with his earlier Prohibitionist Party zeal—Hicks claimed that the culturally accepted religion of his own time was no Christianity at all. The more popular the church became the less Christian it was: "it suffers most when the world treats it best."[25] It appears he may have had this writing in mind years later when he took great pains to claim for Socialism a purely political and secular nature. The goals of a cooperative commonwealth in no way sought to save souls but only to regulate economic behavior.

A year later found Hicks denouncing the next conflict, the U.S.-Filipino War. He rejected any evidence for America's *bona fides* as a Christian nation despite it being "of all the nations on the earth . . . loudest in the boast." Hicks believed that if not for dishonest leadership the "vast majority" of Americans would figure out for themselves the "moral impossibility" of America's take-over of the Philippines. After pointing out the irony of the US fight against the Filipino independence movement, Hicks went to work on his fellow Methodist, Pres. William McKinley:

> If I were a Mohammedan, or a pagan bowing before gods of wood and stone, I would point to the Christian's Bible which says "All things whatsoever ye would that men should do to you, do you even so to them," and then to the so-called Christian president and cabinet of the United States . . . and then to the sickening slaughter of the human beings in the Philippine

Islands . . . and then thank my god, whoever or whatever he might be, that I was not as other men are."²⁶

The turn of the twentieth century found Hicks politically homeless with Populist demise. While still working his day-job at the *West Texas Baptist* he started up a small newspaper of his own to tout the brand-new Farmers' Union just born in Rains County. This paper he called *The Farmers' Journal* and it was the direct predecessor of the largest Socialist newspaper in Texas. As others have shown, the Farmers' Union soon devolved into a power struggle between "actual farmers" and landlords. Choosing sides in that fight was no contest for Hicks, although he still had no political party with which to identify. Nevertheless, his powerful optimism about the possibilities for human society remained strong. He believed that "generations of the future will live in an era of good will and justice and happiness and peace such as the world has never known." The first year of the new century nearly killed Hicks; he came down with typhoid fever and could not work for weeks. In the interim, his fifteen- and-twelve-years-old sons, apparently already apprentices, filled in for him at the *West Texas Baptist* print shop.²⁷

Hicks' journey continued toward a class-conscious critique of the new Texas political economy taking shape around him. He viewed the 1902 poll tax proposal with alarm and wanted everyone to know that "the true object of the poll tax" was simply "disfranchisement." This was in marked contrast to some of the more ambitious former Populist politicians who earned their way back into the Democrats' good graces by embracing racial disfranchisement.²⁸

Hicks' *Farmers' Journal* more or less held its own from 1904 to 1911. He slowly gave up on organized religion while retaining some belief in "an afterlife." At some point in the first decade of the twentieth century, he joined the new Texas Socialist Party. Founded in Bonham in 1898 by a radical ex-populist, the independent Texas party joined with Eugene Debs' Social Democracy in 1900 and combined with other groups in 1901 to become the Socialist Party of America. Hicks had denied being a member of that party in 1901, but its class-conscious message drew him thereafter. By 1908, he was proclaiming his allegiance to the Debsian party in the pages of his paper. By then Hicks had a sufficiently large readership that "Colonel" Dick Maples approvingly noted his conversion in the pages of the *National Rip-Saw*.²⁹

Shortly thereafter, he handed over *The Farmers' Journal* to an enterprising trio from Hallettsville, father-and-son E. O. and E. R. Meitzen, and IWW agitator and Irish immigrant Thomas A. Hickey.

Some controversy clouded this transaction. Davidson and James R. Green present it as a buy-out or merger. The Abilene newspaper reported that Hicks would stay on and regularly contribute a page. Indeed, this was true for the first few months of *The Rebel's* storied run. His weekly feature, "Hicks' Page" pursued Socialist themes of interest to rural Texans. He made a careful case for Socialism's accessibility to believers and non-believers alike, arguing that when understood correctly it was a secular and religiously neutral vehicle for social justice. Accordingly, you could be devout and be a good Socialist or you could be an atheist and be a good Socialist. "But you can't be a Socialist and believe that any individual should have to pay any other individual for the use of the soil to make a living. Keep your Socialism on straight."[30]

Having dispensed with religious controversy, Hicks moved on to another sore topic. In spite of cultural aspirations to the contrary, on small farms much of the cotton production required the labor of women and children. He asked over four dozen "reliable farmers" to estimate the portion of the cotton crop resulting from the labor "of women, and their little children who ought to be in school" and reported--with obvious moral outrage—that his farmers self-reported an average of 53 percent. This appeared in midsummer, 1911.[31]

Then "Hicks' Page" abruptly ended and never returned. From the pages of the *Texarkana Socialist*, the nationally known Texas writer Nat L. Hardy opined that Hickey and the Meitzens cheated Hicks. "They took J. L. Hicks' subscription list and gave him in exchange a ten-dollar-a-week job. But J. L. Hicks is an honest man and has trust in his fellows and therefore did not bind Hickey and Meitzen with a written contract and after six months they fired Hicks without notice."[32]

Dissolving his relationship with *The Rebel* appears not to have slowed down Hicks' agitation for Socialism even a little. During his last years in Abilene he contributed columns extolling the virtues of Socialism in numerous small-town and rural Texas newspapers and continued his commentary on all things Abilene in letters to the Abilene Reporter. Hicks scolded the *Abilene Reporter* for inviting only members of the "25,000 Club," the city's "heaviest tax payers," to express their opinions regarding a new city charter. He contended the newspaper was "asking the man who won in the game to name the rules under which the loser must continue to play." Worse yet, such elitism contradicted "Jefferson's democratic ideals." The *Reporter* printed Hicks' critique but did not spare him in its reply. "Mr. Hicks is an expert at creating mountains out of mole hills . . . . For years Mr. Hicks has stood as the champion of the laboring man, particularly the man whose taxes is confined to the amount of a poll tax receipt." The *Reporter* writer, surely a younger man, took a gratuitous swipe at Hicks as someone old enough to know better because he "is no spring chicken." The Hicks family had been in Abilene for over twenty years and Joshua Hicks was now 54 years old. Soon, he would be moving again.[33]

Lured to Waco by the prospect of starting a new—and short-lived—publication, he and his family stayed on after he obtained a new job with the *Waco Times-Herald* as a printer and proofreader.[34] Hicks would spend almost all of the last decade of his life in Waco. This freethinking Socialist would not have seen the irony of making his home in the Lone Star Vatican. He had long admired Reddin Andrews, the two-time Socialist nominee for Texas governor, and Andrews was as good a Baptist as you could be—a graduate of Southern Seminary, an ordained pastor, and former president of Baylor, no less. And Hicks loved him so much he named his youngest daughter after him.[35]

Waco brought its heartaches. His second oldest child died shortly after their arrival. She was twenty-nine, single, and lived at home. Another daughter was deaf and could not speak; she would never leave the family home. The other six children grew up, married, and moved on. He took obvious pride in his sons. Two went into typographical work and one, Louis Hicks, became prominent in the twentieth-century Texas labor movement.[36]

The propaganda build-up to the U.S. entry into World War I found Hicks sticking to his old pacifist position. To Waco's many pastors he wryly observed that perhaps before they joined the President's preparedness campaign they should be aware that "there seems to be some contrast between Wilson's peace program and that of Isaiah" with America's plowshares being beaten into swords.[37]

Years after the zenith of Texas Socialism waned and former radicals like the Meitzens and Tom Hickey moved into new ventures, Hicks kept the faith. In 1919, he engaged the editor of the *Waco Times-Herald* in a vigorous debate over which system best protected individualism, capitalism or Socialism. The *Times-Herald* asserted that it chose individualism over Socialism, and the editor challenged Hicks to state why capitalism was not individualism. Hicks began with an orthodox definition of democratic socialism but moved on to a more imaginative argument claiming for Socialism "freer and more unshackled individualism." Hicks argued that when the capitalist system established laws allowing one man to determine whether to hire or fire a thousand men, "to feed them out of the products of their own labor or starve them by withholding those products" then, there was capitalism but not individualism. The *Times-Herald* called Hicks "beloved brother" and observed patronizingly that he "discusses every question in fine spirit and to intelligent purpose" and that "we recognize in Mr. Hicks one who loves his fellow-man" before roundly rejecting his arguments with a rebuttal from Hicks' own eighteenth century hero: "'That government is best that governs least.'"[38]

Hicks kept on writing and preaching his radical gospel of Socialism, nonviolence, female suffrage and the brotherhood of man during his last years in Waco.[39] His final year he spent in Dallas. He and his wife moved to the northern metropolis to be near their sons, Jesse and Louis, both typesetters and union activists. He had been a night sky-watcher for decades and his amateur astronomical reading and observations seemed to increase as he aged. This did not, however, diminish his zeal in fighting for the working class. Seven months before he died, he denounced the rise of Dallas' open shop movement in the pages of the *Dallas Craftsman*. "'Open shop' may sound nice to the general public," he wrote, "but its real meaning" is that the union hall will be henceforth will be "closed tight forever." "It means that the lone individual worker, unidentified with any other worker in the whole wide world, shall go to a closed corporation shop and make an entirely one-sided bargain for a job by which to keep from starving to death."[40] Less than three weeks before he died he sent one last epistle out into posterity: "Sooner or later the world will have to come to public ownership of its basic industries as the only remedy for inequality and inequity of distribution." This appeared on October 11, 1921. Eighteen days later he died.[41]

Three years before he died, he wrote one last poem contrasting his love for the night sky and for astronomy to the war-and-pain-wracked earth below it. In spite of the earth's "stench of death," "blast and explosion and broken wings," and his "aching wonder ("Oh! Why these things?"), the aging ex-farmer and print shop worker comforted himself with this prospect:

> Night wind, blow the smoke from beneath these stars;
> Let me see Vega, Capella and Mars
> Their glitter and gleam and majestic sweep
> Drive away all thought of the things that creep
> They are singing love's sweet, celestial song.
> I have looked at the earth too long.[42]

NOTES

1. In my first encounter with Joshua L. Hicks, I missed the importance of the changing nature of his spiritual journey and ascribed 1880s-1890s motives to his 1910s writings. His final adoption of the Socialist Party occurred after he left the church. Several years later, Hicks articulated a belief in Socialism's secular utility based in a rational search for a more just and humane society without regard to religious belief. Nevertheless, his roots in primitive Christianity, with its intimations of human equality, remained an influence. Kyle Wilkison, *Yeomen, Sharecroppers and Socialists: Plain Folk Protest in Texas, 1870-1914* (College Station: Texas A&M University Press, 2008), p. 141; Joshua Hicks, "Hicks' Page," *Rebel* (Hallettsville, TX), July 1, 1911, p. 4.

2. Lawrence Goodwyn, *Democratic Promise: The Populist Movement in America* (New York: Oxford University Press, 1976); James R. Green, *Grass-Roots Socialism: Radical Movements in the Southwest, 1895-1943* (Baton Rouge: Louisiana State University Press, 1978); Chandler Davidson, *Race and Class in Texas Politics* (Princeton, NJ: Princeton University Press, 1990); Kevin D. Williamson, "Chaos in the Family, Chaos in the State: The White Working Class's Dysfunction," *National Review*, March 17, 2016, http://www.nationalreview.com/article/432876/donald-trump-white-working-class-dysfunction-real-opportunity-needed-not-trump; Nancy Isenberg, *White Trash: The 400-Year Untold History of Class in America* (New York: Viking, 2016); Thomas Sowell, *Black Rednecks and White Liberals* (New York: Encounter Books, 2006); for the racialization of Texas elites' contempt for the white working class, see Michael Phillips, *White Metropolis: Race, Ethnicity, and Religion in Dallas, 1841-2001* (Austin: University of Texas Press, 2006) and Neil Foley, *White Scourge: Mexicans, Blacks, and Poor Whites in Texas Cotton Culture* (Berkeley: University of California Press, 1999); for an example of painting with a broadly stereotypical brush, see Michael McGerr, *A Fierce Discontent: The Rise and Fall of the Progressive Movement in America, 1870-1920* (New York: Free Press, 2003), p. 27; for a recent example of the "culture in crisis" explanation, see J.D. Vance, *Hillbilly Elegy: A Memoir of a Family and Culture in Crisis* (New York: Harper Collins, 2016).

3. Hicks Family Papers AR228, Box 1, Folder 228-1-1, Special Collections, The University of Texas at Arlington Library.

4. "Clarke County," *Encyclopedia of Alabama*, http://www.encyclopediaofalabama.org/article/h-1204 (accessed October 10, 2016); Joshua L. Hicks, "Family Record" loose leaf typescript, Scrapbook 1, Hicks Family Papers, AR228, Box 1, Folder 228-1-1, Special Collections, The University of Texas at Arlington Library [hereafter Scrapbook 1 or Scrapbook 2 with page numbers]; Clarke County, Alabama, Manuscript Census, Ninth Census of the United States, 1870; T.H. Ball, *A glance into the great South-east, or, Clarke County, Alabama and its surroundings: from 1540-1877* (Grove Hill, Alabama, 1882), pp. 354-355; Scrapbook 1, pp. 297 and 227.

5. Hopkins County, Texas, Manuscript Census, Tenth Census of the United States, 1880; Scrapbook 1, p. 249.

6. Untitled love poem to his future wife dated September 12, 1880, two years before their marriage. Front matter loose leaf scraps in Scrapbook 1.

7. "Family Record" front matter loose leaf typescript, Scrapbook 1.

8. "How Strange," *The Patron of Husbandry* (Columbus, MS), August 5, 1882, p. 2.

9. *Handbook of Texas Online*, Travis L. Summerlin, "Cranfill, James Britton Buchanan Boone," http://www.tshaonline.org/handbook/online/articles/fcr07 (accessed October 5, 2016).

10. Scrapbook 1, pp. 153-154.

11. Scrapbook 1 p 155.

12. Davidson, xxvii; "As to Race Equality," *American Socialist*, clipping, Scrapbook 1, p. 245.

13. Davidson writes that he searched in vain for any commentary from Hicks on the Waco Horror or on race in general after 1915, but it is clear that his 1918 "Mob" piece was indirectly responding to his struggle to understand the horrifying behavior of his neighbors in the lynch mob death of Jesse Washington. "When the Mob Gets Started," *Waco Times-Herald*, April 17, 1918; Scrapbook 1, p. 283.

14. Scrapbook 1, p. 10.

15. Scrapbook 1, p 18.

16. Scrapbook 1, pp. 19-23.

17. Scrapbook 1, p. 161.

18. Scrapbook 1, p. 176.

19. Scrapbook 1, pp. 177-179.

20. Scrapbook 1, p. 196.

21. Lawrence Goodwin, *The Populist Moment: A Short History of the Agrarian Revolt in America* (London: Oxford University Press, 1978), pp. 215-220; Scrapbook 1, pp. 183 and 188-189; Scrapbook 2, pp. 15 and 28.

22. Scrapbook 1, p. 193.

23. Davidson, p. xxiv.

24. Scrapbook 1, p. 178.

25. Joshua L. Hicks, *Christianity, War, and Politics: Can a Man be a Christian and Kill his Fellow Man?* (Abilene: J.L. Hicks, 1898), pp. 3 and 18-19; Folder AR228-1-11, Hicks Papers.

26. Scrapbook 1, pp. 203-204.

27. "Former Resident of Abilene Dies at Dallas," *Abilene Daily Reporter* (Abilene, TX), Vol. 34, No. 256, Ed. 1, November 1, 1921, p. 3; James Bissett, *Agrarian Socialism in America: Marx, Jefferson, and Jesus in the Oklahoma Countryside, 1904-1920* (Norman: University of Oklahoma Press, 1999); Scrapbook 1, 208-210.

28. Scrapbook 2, p. 78; Robert Worth Miller, "Building a Progressive Coalition in Texas: The Populist Reform Democrat Rapprochement, 1900-1907," *Journal of Southern History* 52 (May 1986): pp. 163-182.

29. *Abilene Daily Reporter*, November 1, 1921, p. 3; Davidson, p. xxv; Scrapbook 1, pp. 208 and 219.

30. "Hicks' Page," *The Rebel* (Hallettsville, TX), July 1, 1911, p. 4.

31. "Hicks' Page," July 22, 1911, p. 4.

32. Scrapbook 1, p. 221; Green, p. 138; Davidson, p. xxv; Scrapbook 2, p. 103.

33. Scrapbook 1, pp. 221-222.

34. *Abilene Daily Reporter*, November 1, 1921, p. 3.

35. "Family Record," Scrapbook 1.

36. "Mathews Family History Exchange," https://mathewsfamilyhistory.files.wordpress.com/2015/02/chart_-clarke-co-mathews-3-gen-4-2007-8-x-11pdf (accessed November 26, 2016); Scrapbook 1 and 2.

37. Hicks, "Christ's Attitude on Defense," *Waco Morning News*, March 3, 1916, clipping; Scrapbook 2, n.p.

38. Scrapbook 1, pp. 269-273.

39. Scrapbook 1, p. 323; Wilkison, pp. 140-143.

40. Scrapbook 1, p. 288.

41. Scrapbook 2, p. 61.

42. Scrapbook 1, p. 258.

www.ingramcontent.com/pod-product-compliance
Lightning Source LLC
Chambersburg PA
CBHW030522080526
44586CB00011B/297